ESCHATOLOGY

OR

THE CATHOLIC DOCTRINE OF
THE LAST THINGS

A DOGMATIC TREATISE

BY

THE RT. REV. MSGR. JOSEPH POHLE, Ph.D., D.D.

FORMERLY PROFESSOR OF APOLOGETICS AT THE CATHOLIC
UNIVERSITY OF AMERICA

AUTHORIZED ENGLISH VERSION WITH SOME ABRIDGMENT
AND ADDITIONAL REFERENCES

BY

ARTHUR PREUSS

GREENWOOD PRESS, PUBLISHERS
WESTPORT, CONNECTICUT

BT
821
.P6413
1971

Originally published in 1917
by B. Herder Book Company, St. Louis, Mo., and London

First Greenwood Reprinting 1971

Library of Congress Catalogue Card Number 72-109823

SBN 8371-4314-4

Printed in the United States of America

TABLE OF CONTENTS

INTRODUCTION

1. DEFINITION.—Eschatology is the crown and capstone of dogmatic theology. It may be defined as "the doctrine of the last things," and tells how the creatures called into being and raised to the supernatural state by God, find their last end in Him, of whom, and by whom, and in whom, as Holy Scripture says, "are all things." [1]

Eschatology is anthropological and cosmological rather than theological; for, though it deals with God as the Consummator and Universal Judge, strictly speaking its subject is the created universe, *i. e.* man and the cosmos.

The consummation of the world is not left to "fate" (*fatum, εἱμαρμένη*). God is a just judge, who distinguishes strictly between virtue and vice and metes out reward or punishment to every man according to his deserts. The rational creatures were made without their choice; but they can not reach their final end without their coöperation. Their destiny depends upon the attitude they take towards the divine plan of salvation. The good are eternally rewarded in Heaven, the wicked are punished forever in Hell. In the latter God

1 Rom. XI, 36.

will manifest His justice, while in the former He will show His love and mercy. By dealing justly with both good and bad, He at the same time triumphantly demonstrates His omnipotence, wisdom, and holiness. Thus Eschatology leads us back to the theological principle that the created universe in all its stages serves to glorify God.[2]

The consummation of the world may be regarded either as in process (*in fieri*) or as an accomplished fact (*in facto esse*). Regarding it from the former point of view we speak of the "last things" (*novissima,* τὰ ἔσχατα), *i. e.* the events to happen at the second coming of our Lord. "The four last things of man" are Death, Judgment, Heaven (Purgatory) and Hell.[3]

The four last things of the human race as a whole are: the Last Day, the Resurrection of the Flesh, and the Final Judgment, followed by the End of the World. These four events constitute as many stages on the way to the predestined state of consummation (*consummatio saeculi,* συντέλεια αἰῶνος), which will be permanent and irrevocable.

DIVISION.—In the light of these considerations it is easy to find a suitable division for the present treatise. The object of the final consummation is

---

2 Cfr. Pohle-Preuss, *God the Author of Nature and the Supernatural,* 2nd ed., pp. 80 sqq., St. Louis 1916.
3 Cfr. Ecclus. VII, 40: "*In om-* nibus operibus tuis memorare novissima tua, et in aeternum non peccabis.*"

the created universe, consisting of pure spirits, human beings, and irrational creatures. The lot of the spirits (angels and demons) was determined forever at the very beginning of things.[4] Man and the physical universe still await their consummation. Man, individually as well as collectively, occupies the centre of creation. Hence we may divide Eschatology into two parts: (1) The Eschatology of Man as an Individual, (2) The Eschatology of the Human Race.

GENERAL READINGS:— St. Thomas, *Summa Theologica, Supplementum,* qu. 69 sq.; *Summa contra Gentiles,* III, 1–63 (tr. by Rickaby, *God and His Creatures,* pp. 183–233, London 1905), and the commentators. Mazzella, *De Deo Creante,* disp. 6, 4th ed., Rome 1908.— E. Méric, *L'Autre Vie,* Paris 1880; 12th ed., Paris 1900; (German tr., *Das andere Leben,* Mayence 1882).—*Card. Katschthaler, *Eschatologia,* Ratisbon 1888.— F. Stentrup, S.J., *Soteriologia,* Vol. II, Innsbruck 1889.— Chr. Pesch, S.J., *Praelectiones Dogmaticae,* Vol. IX, 3rd ed., Freiburg 1911.—*Atzberger, *Die christliche Eschatologie in den Stadien ihrer Offenbarung im A. u. N. T.,* Freiburg 1890.— B. Tepe, S.J., *Institutiones Theologicae,* Vol. IV, pp. 680 sqq., Paris 1896.— P. Einig, *De Deo Creante et Consummante,* Treves 1898.— B. Jungmann, *De Novissimis,* 4th ed., Ratisbon 1898.—J. Royer, *Die Eschatologie des Buches Job unter Berücksichtigung der vorexilischen Propheten,* Freiburg 1901.— *W. Schneider, *Das andere Leben; Ernst und Trost der christlichen Weltanschauung,* 10th ed., Paderborn 1910.— Card. Billot, S.J., *Quaestiones de Novissimis,* 3rd ed., Rome 1908.— Prager, *Die Lehre von der Vollendung aller Dinge,* 1903.— Heinrich-Gutberlet, *Dogmatische Theologie,* Vol. X, Part II, Münster 1904.— J. E. Niederhuber, *Die Eschatologie des hl. Ambrosius,* Paderborn 1907.— J. Keel, *Die jenseitige Welt,* 3 vols., Einsiedeln 1868 sqq.— D. Palmieri, S.J., *De Novissimis,* Rome

4 Cfr. Pohle-Preuss, *God the Author of Nature and the Supernatural,* 2nd ed., St. Louis 1916, pp. 340 sqq.

1908.— Wilhelm-Scannell, *A Manual of Catholic Theology*, Vol. II, 2nd ed., pp. 534-560, London 1901.— S. J. Hunter, S.J., *Outlines of Dogmatic Theology*, Vol. III, pp. 424-464, London 1894.— P. J. Toner, art. "Eschatology," in the *Catholic Encyclopedia*, Vol. V, pp. 528-534.— W. O. E. Osterley, *The Doctrine of the Last Things*, London 1908.— M. O'Ryan, "Eschatology of the Old Testament," in the *Irish Ecclesiastical Record*, Vol. XXVII, No. 509, 4th Series, pp. 472-486.— Charles, *Critical History of the Doctrine of a Future Life in Israel, in Judaism, and in Christianity*, London 1899 (to be read with caution).

For further bibliographical data see Alger, *A Critical History of the Doctrine of the Future Life, with Complete Bibliography by Ezra Abbott*, New York 1871.

For the early history of Eschatology see Atzberger, *Die Geschichte der christlichen Eschatologie innerhalb der vornizänischen Zeit*, Freiburg 1896.

PART I

ESCHATOLOGY OF MAN AS AN INDIVIDUAL

CHAPTER I

DEATH

1. DEFINITION OF DEATH.—"Death,"[1] in common as well as Scriptural usage, means the cessation of life.

a) There is a threefold life (physical, spiritual, and eternal), and hence there must be a threefold death.

(1) Physical death consists in the separation of the body from the soul;

(2) Spiritual death is the loss of sanctifying grace, caused by original or mortal sin;[2]

(3) "Eternal death" is a synonym for damnation. St. John[3] calls damnation "the second death;"[4] St. Paul, "eternal punishment,"[5] "corruption,"[6] "destruction."[7]

St. Augustine says: "Though Holy Scripture mentions

---

1 *Mors, θάνατος.*
2 Cfr. *Conc. Trident.,* Sess. V, can. 2: "*peccatum quod est mors animae.*"
3 Apoc. II, 11; XX, 6, 14; XXI, 8.

4 *Mors secunda, δεύτερος θάνατος.*
5 "Ολεθρον αἰώνιον. (2 Thess. I, 9).
6 Φθορά. (Gal. VI, 8).
7 'Απώλεια. (Phil. III. 19).

5

many deaths, there are two principal ones, namely, the
death which the first man [Adam] incurred by sin,
and that which the second man [Christ] will inflict
in the judgment." [8] Here bodily death and the loss
of sanctifying grace are comprised under one term, as an
effect of original sin. Of course, the loss of sanctifying
grace [9] and eternal damnation can be called " death " only
in a figurative sense.

b) Literally death means the cessation of bodily life, caused by the separation of the soul from
the body.[10] It is principally in this sense that
Eschatology is concerned with death.

The Biblical names for death are as various as they are
significant. Some are derived from the symptoms that at-
tend the separation of the soul from the body; e. g. " dissolution," [11] " end," [12] " outcome," [13] " return to the earth," [14]
etc. Others point to original sin as the cause of death;
for instance, " work of the devil," [15] " the enemy," [16]
" what God hath not made," [17] etc. Belief in immortality
is more or less evident from such phrases as " sleep," [18]
stripping off the earthly house of habitation,[19] the " lay-
ing away of this tabernacle," [20] going to the fathers,[21]

---

8 *Opus Imperfect. c. Iulian.*, VI,
31: " *Quamvis multae mortes in-
veniantur in Scripturis, duae sunt
praecipuae: prima et secunda; prima
est quam peccando intulit primus
homo [Adam], secunda est quam
iudicando illaturus est secundus
homo [Christus].*"

9 Ἁμαρτία πρὸς θάνατον. (Cfr.
I John V, 16).

10 Cfr. St. Augustine, *De Civ. Dei*,
XIII, 6: " *separatio animae a cor-
pore.*"— Clement of Alexandria,
Stromata, 7 (Migne, *P. G.*, IX, 500):

ὁ θάνατος . . . χωρισμὸς ψυχῆς
ἀπὸ σώματος.

11 Phil. I, 23; 2 Tim. IV, 6.

12 Matth. X, 22.

13 Heb. XIII, 7.

14 Gen. III, 19.

15 John VIII, 44.

16 1 Cor. XV, 26.

17 Wisd. I, 13.

18 Job III, 13; Ps. XII, 4; Matth.
IX, 24.

19 2 Cor. V, 1.

20 2 Pet. I, 14.

21 Gen. XV, 15 and elsewhere.

resting from labor,[22] the return of the spirit to God.[23] The latter class of appellations is by far the most important, since it presupposes belief in the immortality of the soul. While the body decays or returns to the dust from which it was formed, the soul lives on for ever. Its separation from the body is merely temporary: at the general Resurrection the two will be reunited.[24]

The state of the soul after its separation from, and until its reunion with, the body must not be conceived as an unconscious dream or a sort of semi-conscious "soul-sleep" (hypnopsychy, psychopannychy), but as a purely spiritual life, accompanied by full consciousness and determined as to happiness or unhappiness by the result of the particular judgment held immediately after death.[25]

2. THE DOGMATIC TEACHING OF THE CHURCH. —Divine Revelation teaches that:

(1) Death is universal;

(2) It is a result of sin; and

(3) It ends the state of probation.

Thesis I: Death is universal.

This proposition embodies the common teaching of Catholic theologians.

Proof. That death is universal we know from experience. Furthermore reason tells us that it is natural for man to be separated into his constituent elements, body and soul.

a) Physiology teaches that every body contains within itself the germs of dissolution and hence is doomed to die.

---

22 Apoc. XIV, 13.
23 Eccles. XII, 7.
24 V. infra, Part II, Ch. II.
25 V. infra, Sect. 2, pp. 22 sqq.

When death comes as the result of old age, it is called "natural" or "physiological."[26] Sacred Scripture expresses a fact of ordinary and universal experience when it calls death "the way of all the earth"[27] and teaches that "It is appointed unto men once to die."[28] Not even Christ and His Immaculate Mother were exempt from death.

b) Certain exceptional cases reported in Sacred Scripture give rise to the question whether the universality of death is metaphysical or merely moral, in other words, whether all men must die, or whether some escape the ordinary fate of mankind.

a) Thus we are told that Henoch, the father of Mathusala, "was translated, that he should not see death;"[29] he "walked with God, and was seen no more, because God took him."[30]

Of Elias the prophet we read that, as he and his friend Eliseus were walking and talking together, "a fiery chariot and fiery horses parted them both asunder, and Elias went up by a whirlwind into heaven."[31]

It seems certain that these two men are, as St. Augustine puts it, still "living in the same bodies in which they were born."[32] But there is no reason to suppose that they will escape the law of death. Since Tertullian's time it has been a pious belief among Christians that Enoch and Elias are the two witnesses mentioned in the Apocalypse,[33] that they will reappear at the end of the

---

26 Cfr. H. Kisbert, *Der Tod aus Altersschwäche*, Bonn 1908; Flint, *Human Physiology*, p. 849, New York 1888.

27 Jos. XXIII, 14; 3 Kings II, 2.

28 Heb. IX, 27: "*Statutum est hominibus semel mori.*" Cfr. Ps. LXXXVIII, 49: "*Quis est homo, qui vivet et non videbit mortem?*"

29 Heb. XI, 5.

30 Cfr. Gen. V, 24; Ecclus. XLIV, 16; XLIX, 16.

31 4 Kings II, 11.

32 *De Peccato Originali*, II, 24: "*Eliam et Henoch non dubitamus, in quibus nati sunt corporibus, vivere.*"

33 Apoc. XI, 3 sqq.

world to preach penance and finally be "overcome by the beast," *i. e.* die as martyrs to the faith.[34]

β) Concerning the just who will survive on earth at the second coming of our Lord, St. Paul teaches: "Behold I tell you a mystery: we shall not all fall asleep, but we shall all be changed."[35] The Vulgate renders this passage differently: "We shall all rise again, but we shall not all be changed."[36] But the Greek text has in its favor the famous Vatican codex, most of the uncial and practically all the cursive manuscripts and vernacular versions.[37] Besides, the reading we have adopted is

[34] Cfr. Tertullian, *De Anima*, 50: "*Nec mors eorum reperta est, dilata scil.; ceterum morituri reservantur, ut Antichristum sanguine suo extinguant.*" (Migne, *P. L.*, II, 735). However, as this interpretation is contradicted by St. Jerome (*Ep. 119 ad Minerv. et Alex.*, n. 4) and others, it is not entirely certain.

[35] 1 Cor. XV, 51: Πάντες μὲν οὐ κοιμηθησόμεθα, πάντες δὲ ἀλλαγησόμεθα.

[36] "*Omnes quidem resurgemus, sed non omnes immutabimur.*"

[37] Cfr. C. Lattey, S.J., in the Appendix to the Westminster Version of 1 Cor.; Cornely, *Comment. in 1 Cor.*, pp. 506 sqq., Paris 1890; Al. Schäfer, *Erklärung der beiden Briefe an die Korinther*, pp. 334 sqq., Münster 1903; J. MacRory, *The Epistles of St. Paul to the Corinthians*, P. I, pp. 251 sqq., Dublin 1915. Speaking of the reading which we have adopted, Dr. MacRory (p. 252 sq.) says: "It is supported by B E K L P among uncials, by nearly all the cursive MSS., by the Syriac, Coptic, Gothic versions, as well as by many MSS. of the Aethiopic; it was the reading of not a few Latin MSS. in the time of St. Jerome, and it is the reading known

to practically all the Greek Fathers. On the ground of external evidence, therefore, this reading is far the most probable. But internal evidence is almost more in its favor, for according to this reading (a) there is a mystery here, namely, that some shall be changed and put on immortality without passing through death, (b) the Apostle, as in the rest of the chapter, refers only to the just, either all the just of all times if we render: 'we shall not all sleep'; or all the just alive at the Second Coming if we render: none of us shall sleep'; (c) the connexion with the next verse is easy and natural: we shall not all die but we shall all be changed in a moment,' etc. We take it, then, that this is the true reading. Nor need there be difficulty about admitting an error in our Vulgate about even a dogmatic text like this, the reading of which was uncertain not only at the time of the Council of Trent but even in the days of St. Jerome. Trent, indeed, binds us to receive as sacred and canonical the sacred books with all their parts, as they were wont to be read in the Catholic Church and are contained in the Old Latin Vulgate (Sess. iv, Decr.

demanded by the context. " In the previous verse," says
Father Lattey, " St. Paul lays it down that the body in
its present perishable condition cannot enter heaven. At
once the difficulty arises about the just who are alive at
the last day. St. Paul meets it by telling of a ' mystery ';
these just, it is true, will not die, but none the less their
bodies will have to be glorified — *all* the just, living or
dead, will be *changed*. When the *dead* rise incorruptible,
we, the living, shall be *changed; * our corruptible bodies
will put on incorruption. After that supreme moment,
death will have lost all power over man; human bodies
will be perishable no more." [38]

This plausible interpretation is confirmed by the following passage in Saint Paul's First Epistle to the
Thessalonians: " For this we tell you as the Lord's
word, that we who live, who survive until the Lord's
coming, shall not precede them that are fallen asleep
(*dormierunt*), . . . and the dead in Christ shall rise
first (*primi*, πρῶτον). Thereupon (*deinde*) we the
living, who remain, shall together with them be caught up
(*simul rapiemur cum illis*) in the clouds to meet the
Lord in the air, and thus we shall be ever with the
Lord." [39]

It is but fair to add, however, that these two Pauline
texts have been variously interpreted. St. Chrysostom,
St. Jerome, and apparently also Tertullian,[40] taught that
the just who survive on the last day shall be glorified
without having died. St. Ambrose, St. Augustine, and

de can. script.). But the Vulgate
version of this verse was never read
throughout the Catholic Church, being apparently unknown in the
East, and hence even if the single
verse be a part ' of Scripture in
the sense intended by the Council,
we are free to reject the Vulgate
reading of it. (Cf. Corn., *Introd.
Gen.*, p. 456 ff.; *Compend.*, p. 114
ff.)."

[38] Cfr. C. Lattey, Appendix I to 1
Cor., p. 52.

[39] 1 Thess. IV, 14 sqq. (Westminster Version).

[40] *De Resurrectione Carnis*, 41,
42.

others held that they shall die and slumber a while before being summoned to the Last Judgment. The majority of Catholic divines, in view of St. Paul's teaching that all who have sinned in Adam must die,[41] prefer to steer a middle course.[42] They hold that while all men must die, some will survive until immediately before the General Judgment. This teaching is favored by the Roman Catechism [43] and many modern exegetes.

c) Whichever opinion one may prefer in regard to the question here at issue, it is certain that even if Henoch and Elias did not and never will die, the debt of death (*debitum mortis*) rests upon all the descendants of Adam. "It is held with greater probability and more commonly," says St. Thomas, "that all those who are alive at the coming of our Lord, will die and rise again after a short while. . . . If, however, it be true, as others hold, that they will never die, . . . then we must say . . . that although they are not to die, the debt of death is none the less in them, and that the punishment of death will be remitted by God, since He can also forgive the punishment due for actual sins." [44] The only human beings ex-

41 Cfr. Rom. V, 12 sqq.
42 Cfr. Oecumenius, in Migne, P. G., CXVIII, 894: "*Istud 'non omnes dormiemus' hoc modo oportet accipere quod non dormiemus diuturnâ dormitione (τὴν χρονικὴν κοίμησιν), ut opus sit sepulchro ac solutione ad corruptionem; sed brevem mortem sustinebunt, qui tunc reperientur.*"

43 P. I, c. 12, qu. 4.
44 *Summa Theologica*, 1a 2ae, qu. 81, art. 3, ad 1: "*Probabilius et convenientius tenetur, quod omnes illi qui in adventu Domini reperientur, morientur et post modicum resurgent. . . . Si tamen hoc verum sit, quod alii dicunt, quod illi nunquam morientur, dicendum est quod . . . est tamen in eis reatus mortis.*"

empt from this law are Jesus Christ and His blessed Mother, though they too, actually paid tribute to death.

Thesis II: Death in the present economy is a punishment for sin.

This proposition embodies an article of faith.

Proof. It is the dogmatically defined teaching of the Church that our first parents were endowed with bodily immortality,[45] but lost this prerogative for themselves and their descendants through sin.[46]

God solemnly forbade Adam and Eve to eat of the fruit of a certain tree. "In what day soever thou shalt eat of it, thou shalt die the death." [47] By transgressing this command our first parents incurred death. Thus, in the words of the Apostle, "by one man sin entered into this world, and by sin death; and so death passed upon all men, in whom all have sinned." [48]   Therefore, "the wages of sin is death." [49]

Long before St. Augustine, as the latter assured Julian,[50] the Fathers considered the causal connection between sin and death to be an article of faith.[51]

Sed poena aufertur a Deo, qui etiam peccatorum actualium poenas condonare potest."
45 Cfr. *Syn. Milev.*, A. D. 416, can. 1.
46 Cfr. *Syn. Arausic.* II, can. 2; *Conc. Trident.*, Sess. V, can. 2.

47 Gen. II, 17; cfr. Gen. III, 19.
48 Rom. V, 12.
49 Rom. VI, 23; cfr. 1 Cor. XV, 21, 22.
50 *Contra Iulian.*, l. II.
51 For the teaching of the Fathers on this point see Ginella, *De No-*

The atonement wiped out sin and thereby enabled man to escape the "second death," *i. e.* eternal damnation. But the gift of bodily immortality was not restored.[52] It is true death loses the character of a punishment through Baptism, because, in the words of the Tridentine Fathers, " there is no condemnation to those who are truly buried together with Christ by Baptism into death." [53] But the *debitum mortis* remains as an effect of sin (*poenalitas*), which God wisely allows for the purification of the just. Only in the case of Christ and His Blessed Mother death was neither a punishment (*poena*) nor an effect of sin (*poenalitas*).[54]

Thesis III: Death ends the state of probation, that is, after death man can neither merit nor demerit.

This thesis embodies what is technically called *"doctrina catholica."*

Proof. Death ends the state of pilgrimage (*status viae*) and inaugurates the state of final consummation (*status termini*), which by its very definition excludes the possibility of further merit or demerit. It is true we cannot prove that this must necessarily be so; but we know it *is* so by virtue of a positive divine law.[55]

The impossibility of acquiring merits after death must

---

tione atque Origine Mortis, § 9, Breslau 1868; for the post-Augustinian period, cfr. Casini, *Quid est Homo?*, ed. Scheeben, pp. 59 sqq., Mayence 1862.— See also Pohle-Preuss, *God the Author of Nature and the Supernatural,* pp. 286 sqq.

[52] Cfr. Rom. V, 18 sqq.

[53] *Conc. Trident.*, Sess. V, can. 5.

[54] See Pohle-Preuss, *Christology,* pp. 72 sqq., and *Mariology,* pp. 72 sqq.

[55] That this law is both congruous and in accordance with nature is convincingly shown by Ripalda, *De Ente Supernaturali,* disp. 77.

not, however, be conceived as a cessation of free will. At their entrance into the *status termini* the Elect as well as the damned once for all decide either for or against God; but within the state thus definitively chosen, each retains full liberty of action.

a) As Christ ceased to acquire merits after His death, so *a fortiori* will man. Death inaugurates "the night when no man can work." [56] Ecclesiastes compares man in this respect with a tree: "If the tree fall to the south, or to the north, in what place soever it shall fall, there shall it be." [57] St. Paul [58] says every man will be judged according as he hath done good or evil "in the body." [59] St. Cyprian teaches that no one can do penance or make satisfaction after death. [60] St. Augustine declares: "It is in this life that all merit or demerit is acquired. . . . No one, then, need hope that he shall obtain after death that which he has neglected to secure here." [61] The Catholic Church has embodied this revealed doctrine in her dogma of the Particular Judgment. [62]

---

56 Cfr. John IX, 4; Matth. XXIV, 42; XXV, 13.

57 Eccles. XI, 3: "*Si ceciderit lignum ad austrum aut ad aquilonem, in quocunque loco ceciderit, ibit erit.*"

58 2 Cor. V, 10.

59 τὰ διὰ τοῦ σώματος.

60 *Ad Demetr.*, 25: "*Quando isthinc excessum fuerit, nullus iam poenitentiae locus, nullus satisfac-* tionis effectus: hic vita aut amittitur aut tenetur.*"

61 *Enchiridion,* c. 110: "*Nemo se speret, quod hic neglexerit, quum obierit, apud Deum promereri.*"— The unanimous teaching of theologians on this point is well developed by Ripalda, *De Ente Supernaturali,* disp. 77, sect. 1 sqq.

62 See *infra,* Ch. 2, pp. 18 sqq.

b) It is the opinion of St. Bonaventure, Ripalda, and Vasquez that the Elect in Heaven and the poor souls in Purgatory can merit and apply for the benefit of others certain *praemia accidentalia*. But this assumption is opposed to the analogy of faith. The power of intercession which the just wield in the world beyond is based entirely upon merits previously acquired in the state of pilgrimage.[63]

Hirscher's view that those who have wavered for a long time between God and the world, and finally die in the state of mortal sin, will be allowed to make their final decision in the next world, is contrary to the dogmatic teaching of the Church.[64]

c) From what we have said it follows that nothing is so well calculated to demonstrate the hollowness of the world and to preserve us from becoming unduly attached to it, as the pious consideration of death. Our earthly life is merely a " pilgrimage," [65] a " journey," [66] and we are to make use of the things of this world only in so far as they aid, or at least do not hinder us in attaining our supernatural destiny.[67] There is much in the thought of death to comfort us. Death ends all our sufferings and trials.[68] But the hour when we shall be called hence is uncertain,[69] and therefore we must watch and pray and strive always to be in the state of sanctifying grace. Mortal sin is the only thing that can prevent us from attaining our last end, which is the beatific vision of God.[70] If we are

---

[63] Cfr. St. Thomas, *Comment. in Sent.*, III, dist. 18, qu. 1, art. 2: " *Beati non sunt in statu acquirendi secundum aliquid sui; et ideo nec sibi nec aliis merentur, quia, quod impetrant modo nobis, contingit ex hoc quod prius, dum viverent, meruerunt ut hoc impetrarent.*"

[64] Hirscher's error is refuted by Father Joseph Kleutgen, S.J., in *Die Theologie der Vorzeit*, Vol. II, 2nd ed., pp. 427 sqq., Münster 1872.

[65] 2 Cor. V, 6.

[66] Jos. XXIII, 14; Wisd. III, 3.

[67] Wisd. V, 1 sqq.

[68] 2 Cor. IV, 16 sqq.; Apoc. XIV, 13.

[69] Matth. XXIV, 42; Luke XII, 39 sq., and elsewhere.

[70] Cfr. Luke XXI, 34.

in the state of grace we can face death unflinchingly.[71]
That the fear of death is so deeply ingrained in human nature,[72] is owing partly to sin and partly to the instinct of
self-preservation.[73] The immortality which our first parents enjoyed in Paradise was a free gift and its loss is
a punishment. Death and the fear of death are entirely
natural.[74] Nevertheless, the thought of death should not
discourage, but rather incite us to spend the short span
of existence granted us here below for the benefit of our
own souls and those near and dear to us.[75] We must not,
because life is short, seek sinful pleasures after the example of the ancient pagans, who had no hope of
Heaven.[76] On the other hand, we should not despise
the things of this world. It would be folly to neg-
lect our earthly affairs in order to devote all our time
to works of piety. Every loyal Catholic should, on
the contrary, do his share in advancing the interests of
true progress and culture and thereby help to disprove the
oft-repeated calumny that the Church is inimical to the
world.[77] The more we accomplish in this world, if
we have the right intention, the more confidently may we
meet death. *Ora et labora!* [78]

READINGS: — Ginella, *De Notione atque Origine Mortis*,
Breslau 1868.— Card. Bellarmine, *De Arte bene Moriendi*, 1620

71 Phil. I, 21 sqq.
72 2 Cor. V, 4; Heb. II, 15.
73 Cfr. St. Augustine, *Serm.*, 172,
c. 1: "*Mortem horret non opinio,
sed natura.*"
74 Cfr. St. Thomas, *Summa Theol.*,
1a 2ae, qu. 164, art. 1: "*Mors est
naturalis propter conditionem naturae
et poenalis propter amissionem di-
vini beneficii praeservantis a morte.*"
75 Cfr. Eccles. IX, 10.
76 Cfr. Reisacker, *Der Todesge-
danke bei den Griechen*, Treves

1862; F. Hettinger, *Apologie des
Christentums*, Vol. II, 9th ed., P. 1,
pp. 23 sqq., Freiburg 1907.
77 Cfr. Leo XIII, Encyclical "*Im-
mortale Dei*," Nov. 1, 1885: "*Imo
inertiae desidiaeque inimica Ecclesia
magnopere vult, ut hominum ingenia
uberes ferant exercitatione et culturâ
fructus.*"
78 Cfr. A. A. Cataneo, *Vorberei-
tung auf einen guten Tod*, 3 vols.,
Ratisbon 1888–91; Weber, *Evangelium und Arbeit*, Freiburg 1898.

(German tr., *Die Kunst zu sterben,* by F. Hense, 2nd ed., Paderborn 1888).— C. M. Kaufmann, *Die Jenseitshoffnungen der Griechen und Römer nach den Sepulkralinschriften,* Freiburg 1899.— IDEM, *Die sepulkralen Jenseitsdenkmäler der Antike und des Urchristentums,* Mayence 1900.— S. J. Hunter, S.J., *Outlines of Dogmatic Theology,* Vol. III, pp. 425-429.

CHAPTER II

THE PARTICULAR JUDGMENT

SECTION 1

THE EXISTENCE OF A PARTICULAR JUDGMENT

1. DEFINITION.—By "judgment" we mean the investigation, sentence, and final order of a civil or criminal court. God pronounces judgment upon the soul immediately after its separation from the body. This Judgment is called Particular, to distinguish it from the General Judgment which takes place at the end of the world.

The essential point in the Catholic dogma of the Particular Judgment is that the soul becomes aware of God's final decision immediately after death. In the General Judgment the emphasis rests rather upon the sentence as such. The Particular Judgment is not necessarily a formal sentence. It may be merely a clear perception of guilt or innocence, whereby the soul is moved of its own accord to hasten either to Heaven, or Hell, or Purgatory, according to its deserts.[1] The Scriptural

---

1 Cfr. St. Thomas, *Summa Theol., Supplem.*, qu. 69, art. 2: "*Sicut corpus per gravitatem vel levitatem statim fertur in locum suum, nisi prohibeatur, ita animae soluto vinculo carnis, per quod in statu viae detinebantur, statim praemium consequuntur vel poenam, nisi aliquid impediat. . . . Et quia locus deputatur animabus secundum congruentiam*

18

"Book of Judgment," with its record of good and
evil deeds, is a metaphor,[2] just like the description which
pious writers give of the judgment scene, where the
devil accuses, while the guardian angel either confirms
the accusation or defends his former client.
Where the Particular Judgment will take place no
one knows. Probably each soul is judged on the spot
where it leaves the body. Though Divine Revelation does
not expressly say so, we may assume that the God-man
Jesus Christ will act as judge both at the Particular and
at the General Judgment.[3]

2. PROOF FROM REVELATION.—Sacred Scripture teaches that the fate of each departed soul is
decided before the General Judgment. If this is
so, there must be a Particular preceding the General Judgment. Calvin [4] and the Chiliasts hold
that the fate of the departed souls remains un-
decided till the second coming of Christ. The
Hypnopsychites maintain that these souls spend
the interval between death and the General Resurrection in a state of unconscious or semi-conscious sleep,—a view which, Father Hunter
thinks, is shared by most Protestants who have
any conviction about the matter at all.[5] Eu-

*praemii vel poenae, statim ut anima
absolvitur a corpore, vel in infernum
mergitur vel ad caelos evolat, nisi im-
pediatur aliquo reatu, quo oporteat
evolationem differri, ut prius anima
purgetur."*
2 Cfr. St. Augustine, *De Civitate
Dei*, XX, 14.
3 Cfr. Suarez, *De Myst. Vitae
Christi*, disp. 52, sect. 2: *" Verisi-*

*mile est, in eo instanti animam cogno-
scere sese iudicari et salvari vel
damnari imperio et efficientiâ non
solum Dei, sed etiam hominis
Christi."*
4 *Instit.*, III, 25.
5 Cfr S. J. Hunter, S.J., *Outlines
of Dogmatic Theology*, Vol. III, p.
430.

sebius tells of a strange sect, called Thnetopsychites, who believed that the disembodied souls
await the General Judgment in a state of temporary annihilation.[6] The teaching of the Church
is that the fate of every man is determined some-
time before the General Judgment.[7]

a) St. Paul says: "It is appointed unto men
once to die, and after this the judgment."[8] This
text may be quoted in favor of our thesis, though
it is not conclusive because we do not know for
certain whether the Apostle refers to the Particular or to the General Judgment.[9] A more convincing proof for our dogma is furnished by the
parable of Lazarus, Luke XVI, 22: "And the
rich man also died, and he was buried in hell."
Dives must have been judged before he was punished. The same is true of Judas, who, according
to the sacred writer, "went to his own place."[10]
Ecclesiastes says that the body "returns into its
earth, from whence it was, while the spirit returns to God who gave it."[11]

b) The teaching of the Fathers is in full accord with that of Sacred Scripture. St. Augustine (to quote but one of them) says the departed
souls are judged as they leave the body and before

6 Hist. Eccles., VI, 37.
7 V. infra, Sect. 2.
8 Heb. IX, 27: "Statutum est
hominibus, semel mori, post hoc
(μετὰ δὲ τοῦτο) autem iudicium."

9 Cfr. Estius i. h. l.
10 ". . . ut abiret in locum suum
(εἰς τὸν τόπον τὸν ἴδιον.) Act. I,
25.
11 Eccles. XII, 7.

they appear at the final judgment, which takes place at the end of the world.[12]

A further confirmation of our dogma will be found below in Section 2, where it is shown that the Particular Judgment takes place *immediately after death.* If the fate of the departed souls is determined immediately after death, it follows that they are judged immediately after death.

[12] *De Anima et eius Origine,* II, 4, 8: " *Rectissime et valde salubriter creditur, iudicari animas, quum de corporibus exierint, antequam veniant ad illud iudicium, quo eas oportet iam redditis corporibus iudicari atque in ipsa, in qua hic vixerunt carne, torqueri sive glorificari.*" (Migne, *P. L.,* XLIV, 498).

SECTION 2

WHEN THE PARTICULAR JUDGMENT TAKES PLACE

I. HISTORICAL DEVELOPMENT OF THE DOGMA.
—The Catholic dogma that the soul is judged immediately after death has passed through a long process of clarification in the minds of the faithful. There was no official definition of it by the Church until the Middle Ages.

a) In the primitive Church vague ideas were current in regard to the immediate fate of the departed.

Not to speak of the Chiliasts, the Hypnopsychites, and the Thnetopsychites, even some orthodox writers harbored erroneous notions concerning the fate of the soul after death. Thus St. Justin Martyr seems to have held that the disembodied souls in the interval between death and the General Resurrection enjoy a natural beatitude.[1] St. Irenaeus imagined them dwelling in a sort of paradise (*locus amoenitatis*) distinct from Heaven.[2] Tertullian believed that the martyrs entered into the beatific vision immediately after death.[3] St. Hilary speaks of a temporary imprisonment (*custodia*) of the soul.[4]

It would, however, be wrong to suppose that these Pa-

[1] *Dial.*, 80.
[2] *Adv. Haereses*, V, 31, 2.
[3] *De Anima*, 55.
[4] *In Ps.*, 120, n. 16.

tristic writers erred in regard to the substance of the dogma. There are many passages in their writings which, at least virtually, inculcate the orthodox view, as when they speak of our Lord's descent into Hell and the intercession of the saints.

b) It was the universal belief of the early Christians that the wicked are buried in Hell immediately after death.

The dread sentence, "Depart from me, you cursed, into everlasting fire," [5] was regarded as the confirmation of a previous judgment and an accentuation of the punishment imposed on both the soul and its risen body. In accordance with this ancient belief, Benedict XII defined in his dogmatic Bull "*Benedictus Deus*," A. D. 1336, "that . . . the souls of those who depart this life in the state of mortal sin descend into Hell immediately after death and are there subject to infernal torments." [6]   A similar passage occurs in the profession of faith submitted by the Greek Emperor Michael Palæologus at the Council of Lyons, A. D. 1274,[7] which was embodied in the Decree of Union adopted at Florence, in 1439.[8]

c) The clarification of ideas with regard to the fate of the just proceeded more slowly.

It was believed at an early date that the just, too, are

5 Matth. XXV, 41.

6 "*Definimus quod . . . animae descendentium in actuali peccato mortali mox post mortem suam ad inferna descendunt, ubi poenis infernalibus cruciantur.*" (Denzinger-Bannwart, n. 531).

7 "*Illorum autem animas, qui in mortali peccato vel cum solo originali descendunt, mox [i. e. statim] in infernum descendere, poenis tamen disparibus puniendas.*" (Denzinger-Bannwart, n. 464).

8 The bearing of this dogmatic decision on the lot of unbaptized infants is explained in Pohle-Preuss, *God the Author of Nature and the Supernatural*, pp. 304 sq.

judged immediately after death; but there was uncertainty as to whether they were forthwith admitted to the vision of the Blessed Trinity or enjoyed some inferior kind of beatitude. This uncertainty continued even after the Second Council of Lyons (1274) had declared that "the souls of the just are received immediately into Heaven." [9] As late as 1330 certain Franciscan theologians are said to have taught that the souls of the just enjoy the vision of Christ as man (in forma servi), but that the beatific vision of God (in forma Dei) was reserved until after the Last Judgment. It is but fair to add, however, that Wadding denies this charge against his fellow-religious.[10] If the Franciscans really held the opinion in question, they shared their mistake with Pope John XXII, who about 1331 privately taught the same doctrine.[11] In 1336 Pope Benedict XII, in his aforementioned Bull, defined that those who depart this life in the state of sanctifying grace "behold the divine essence intuitively and face to face." [12] The Council of Florence cleared away the last remaining doubt by adding the words: "They clearly behold God Himself, one and tri-une, as He is." [13]

2. PROOF FROM REVELATION.—Sacred Scripture teaches that the fate of every man is decided immediately after death and that the ulti-

9 " Illorum [scil. iustorum] animas mox in caelum recipi." (Denzinger-Bannwart, n. 464).

10 Annales Minorum, ad annum 1331, 2nd ed., Vol. VII, p. 118.

11 He did not, however, make an ex cathedra decision on the subject, as the opponents of papal infallibility assert. Cfr. Hefele, Conciliengeschichte, Vol. VI, 2nd ed., pp. 522 sqq., Freiburg 1890.

12 ". . . vident divinam essentiam visione intuitivâ et etiam faciali." (Denzinger-Bannwart, n. 531).

13 ". . . et intueri clare ipsum Deum trinum et unum, sicuti est." (Denzinger-Bannwart, n. 693).— Cfr. Pohle-Preuss, God: His Knowability, Essence, and Attributes, 2nd ed., p. 108, St. Louis 1914.

mate condition of the Blessed and the damned respectively is essentially the same before and after the General Resurrection.

a) Ecclus. XI, 28: "It is easy before God in the day of death to reward every one according to his ways."[14]   If God rewards every one according to his deserts "in the day of death," He must send the souls of the just to Heaven and those of the wicked to Hell immediately after their separation from the body. This is confirmed in the parable which says that "the rich man also died, and was buried in Hell."[15]

St. Hilary writes: "Lazarus was carried by angels to the place prepared for the Elect in Abraham's bosom, whereas Dives was buried forthwith in the place of punishment."[16]   St. Gregory the Great teaches: "As beatitude causes the Elect to be glad, so, it is necessary to believe, fire torments the wicked from the day of their death."[17]   St. John Chrysostom expresses the same thought in a striking simile: "As criminals are dragged in chains from jail to the seat of judgment, so the souls of the departed are forthwith brought before that terrible judgment seat, burdened with the various punishments due to their sins."[18]

b) The fate of the just is illustrated by the ex-

---

14 Ecclus. XI, 28: "Quoniam facile est coram Deo in die obitus retribuere unicuique secundum vias suas."
15 Luke XXIII, 43.
16 In Ps., 2, n. 48: "Testes nobis [sunt] evangelicus dives et pauper, quorum unum angeli in sedibus beatorum et in Abrahae sinu locaverunt, alium statim poenae regio [scil. infernum] suscepit."
17 Dial., IV, 28: "Sicut electos beatitudo laetificat, ita credi necesse est quod a die exitus sui ignis reprobos exurat."
18 Hom. in Matth., XIV, n. 4.

ample of Lazarus, who "was carried by the angels into Abraham's bosom" immediately after his demise,[19] and by Christ's promise to the good thief, "This day thou shalt be with me in paradise."[20] The terms "Abraham's bosom" and "paradise," strictly speaking, signify the *limbus Patrum*, but we know that since the Ascension of our Lord the limbo has made way for Heaven. An even more convincing text is 2 Cor. V, 6 sqq.: "We know that, while we are in the body (ἐνδημοῦντες ἐν τῷ σώματι) we are absent from the Lord (ἐκδημοῦμεν ἀπὸ τοῦ κυρίου), for we walk by faith, and not by sight. But we are confident and have a good will to be absent rather from the body and to be present with the Lord." To "be in the body" means to "walk by faith," to "be present with the Lord," to enjoy the beatific vision, for which the Apostle betrays such a keen desire in his Epistle to the Philippians (I, 21 sqq.). The only means of attaining this end is "absence from the body," *i. e.* death. Consequently, according to St. Paul, the Elect enter upon their celestial inheritance immediately after death.

The Fathers held this dogma implicitly rather than explicitly. St. Cyprian says: "What a dignity it is, and what a security, . . . in a moment to close the eyes with which men and the world are looked upon, and at

19 Luke XVI, 22.   20 Luke XXIII, 43.

once to open them to behold God and Christ!"[21] The Acts of the Martyrs and many ancient liturgies testify to the belief of the primitive Church that those who lay down their lives for the true faith immediately enter into Heaven.[22] That the early Christians held the same belief with regard to all the just is evident from the fact that they prayed to other saints besides the martyrs for their intercession in Heaven. Incidentally it may be noted that the dogma with which we are dealing involves another, namely our Lord's descent into Hell. After the death of Christ His soul went down into Limbo to deliver the souls of the just from the temporary punishment they were suffering, and to introduce them to the beatific vision of God.[23] To deny that these souls now enjoy the beatific vision would involve a rejection of the dogma of Christ's descent into Hell.[24]

21 *De Exhort. Martyr.*, n. 13: " *Quanta est dignitas et quanta securitas, . . . claudere in momento oculos, quibus homines videbantur et mundus, et aperiri eosdem statim, ut Deus videatur et Christus.*" 22 Cfr. Coustant, *Praef. ad Opera*

S. Hilarii, § 6, sect. 3, n. 219. 23 Cfr. Pohle-Preuss, *Soteriology,* 2nd ed., pp. 91 sqq., St. Louis 1916. 24 Cfr. H. Hurter, S.J., *Compendium Theol. Dogmat.,* Vol. III, thes. 268.

CHAPTER III

HEAVEN

SECTION 1

THE EXISTENCE OF HEAVEN

1. DEFINITION.—a) Etymologically the Latin word for "Heaven"[1] means the expanse of sky above the earth, which resembles a great dome or arch apparently containing the sun, moon, and stars. The Church employs the term *caelum* to signify the abode of God and the Blessed, with the emphasis upon the *state* rather than the *place* in which they find themselves.

The Bible refers to Heaven both as a place and as a state (eternal life, eternal rest, the kingdom of God, the joy of the Lord, etc.). In the language of St. Paul, to enter into Heaven is to " be present with the Lord,"[2] which can mean nothing else but a spiritual occupation engaging the highest faculties of the soul and culminating in the knowledge and love of God. As Heaven is man's final goal (*status termini*), it must be identical with the beatitude which comes to the created mind from the

---

1 *Caelum* = a   hollow   sphere;   2 2 Cor. V, 8.
Greek, οὐρανός = vault, ceiling.

contemplation and love of the divine essence and perfections (*status beatitudinis*).

b) To arrive at a real, as opposed to the nominal, definition of Heaven, therefore, we must ascertain in what precisely the happiness of the Elect consists.

Boëthius defines Heaven as "a state made perfect by the accumulation of all good things." [3] St. Thomas, as "the ultimate perfection of rational or intellectual nature." [4] These definitions, while correct, are not sufficiently specific, for a "state made perfect by the accumulation of all good things" and the "ultimate perfection of rational nature" need not necessarily be supernatural.

The happiness produced by the knowledge and love of God would not be the same in a natural state of beatitude as it is in Heaven. In proposing to man a supernatural end, the Creator abolished his purely natural destiny, which consisted in an abstractive knowledge and a natural love of God. In the present economy the rational creature has no choice between natural and supernatural beatitude. To miss the latter means to miss both. Hence Heaven, in the Christian sense, must be a state of *supernatural* beatitude.

In what does this supernatural beatitude consist?

c) The supernatural beatitude of Heaven fun-

8 *De Consolatione Philosophiae,*
III, 2: "*Status omnium bonorum
congregatione perfectus.*"

4 "*Ultima perfectio rationalis sive
intellectualis naturae.*" (*Summa
Theol.,* 1a, qu. 62, art. 1).

damentally consists in the intuitive vision of the
Divine Essence (*visio Dei intuitiva*), as opposed
to the purely abstractive and analogical knowledge which man has of God here below.

St. Paul describes the difference between these
two kinds of knowledge as follows: "Now we
see in a mirror, obscurely; but then [we shall see]
face to face. Now I know in part; then shall I
know fully, even as I have been fully known [by
God]." [5] As the Divine Essence subsists in three
distinct Persons, the beatific vision involves an intuitive knowledge of the Trinity. Needless to
say, the human intellect cannot attain to this ex-
alted knowledge by its own power, but requires
for this purpose a special "light of glory." [6]

The intuitive vision of God is essentially *beatific,* that is, it renders man infinitely happy.

Thomists and Scotists have been engaged in
a long-standing controversy on the question
whether beatitude is in the intellect or in the will.
The two views are not incompatible, in fact, it is
only by judiciously combining them that we arrive at the whole truth, *viz.:* that the knowledge
of God is the essence of beatitude, while the love
of God is its form and goal.

5 i Cor. XIII, 12: "*Videmus
nunc per speculum in aenigmate:
tunc autem facie ad faciem. Nunc
cognosco ex parte: tunc autem co-
gnoscam sicut et cognitus sum.*" Cfr.
i John, III, 2: "*Nunc filii Dei
sumus: et nondum apparuit quid*

*erimus. Scimus quoniam, quum
apparuerit, similes ei erimus: quoniam videbimus eum sicuti est.*"
6 *Lumen gloriae.*— On the *lumen
gloriae* see Pohle-Preuss, *God: His
Knowability, Essence, and Attributes,* p. 146.

d) Perfect beatitude must include the will as
well as the intellect. That beatitude is described more often as knowledge than as love
is owing to the fact that whereas the love we
shall have for God in Heaven is substantially
identical with the love we have for Him here on
earth,[7] the knowledge we shall have of Him there
differs essentially from the abstractive and analogical knowledge which is vouchsafed us here.
This does not, however, prevent the *visio beatifica*
from culminating in a rapturous love, free from
imperfection, whereby the creature is made un-
speakably happy (*amor beatificus*). As faith is
transformed into vision and hope changes to possession, love grows perfect and thus man becomes
completely happy.

2. PROOF FROM REVELATION.—Various heretical errors have been current at one time or other
concerning the nature of Heaven. Certain Armenian writers of the fourteenth century claimed
that the Elect know God in an abstractive manner only. The Palamites or Hesychasts, a school
of Greek mystics who flourished about the
same time on Mount Athos, taught that the divine attributes are mere radiations of God's Essence, which become solidified as it were, by taking on the shape of an uncreated light, perceptible to the Blessed by means of bodily vision.[8]

---

7 Cfr. 1 Cor. XIII, 8 sqq.   8 Cfr. Pohle-Preuss, *op. cit.* (note
6), p. 146.

Rosmini all but denied the beatific vision by saying that its object is not the Divine Essence, but God in His relation to the outside world.[9] The question was authoritatively decided by Benedict XII (1336) and the Council of Florence (1439).[10]

a) For the proof from Revelation see Pohle-Preuss, God: His Knowability, Essence, and Attributes, pp. 80 sqq.

b) The beatitude of Heaven would be incomplete if it did not include freedom from evil;—which is but another way of saying that the Blessed can neither suffer pain nor commit sin.

Evil may be physical or moral. Physical evil disturbs the order of nature; moral evil interferes with the law by which God governs the world. Physical evils are, e. g., ignorance, sorrow, pain, sickness, and death. Moral evils: sin and concupiscence (fomes peccati). In Heaven there is neither physical nor moral evil. Cfr. Apoc. VII, 16: "They shall no more hunger nor thirst; the sun shall not oppress them, nor any heat." Apoc. XXI, 4: "And [God] shall wipe away every tear from their eyes, and death shall be no more, neither shall mourning or wailing or pain be any more, because the first things are passed away."

The greatest of all evils is sin, and therefore the Blessed can no longer sin. As this truth was denied by Origen, it requires special proof. In saying that there

9 Prop. Damnat. a Leone XIII, prop. 38–40. The full text of the decree of the Holy Office condemning Rosmini's teaching will be found in Schiffini, Disput. Metaph. Spec., Vol. I, pp. 432 sqq.

10 V. supra, Ch. II, Sect. 2, pp. 23 and 24.

is no pain or sorrow in Heaven the inspired author of the Apocalypse cannot have meant physical sorrow only. Mental sorrow caused by the loss of sanctifying grace is far deeper and keener than mere physical pain. Moreover, the beatitude of Heaven, being eternal, is incompatible with sin. As St. Augustine aptly observes, the happiness of the Elect would be incomplete if it did not exclude sin.[11]

Whether the so-called impeccability of the Blessed in Heaven is due to a purely extrinsic confirmation in grace, or rooted in the essence of the beatific vision, is a controverted question. St. Thomas declares: " They who are already blessed in Heaven, apprehend the object of true happiness as making their happiness and last end: otherwise their desire would not be set at rest in that object, and they would not be blessed and happy. The will of the Blessed, therefore, cannot swerve from the object of true happiness." [12] This constancy of the will is rooted in an ineradicable love of God, which, being based on a true knowledge of His essence, has neither the power nor the will to offend Him.[13] However, there is this much truth in the opposing view of the Scotists, that the beatific vision and impeccability, though connected by an intrinsic natural bond, are not essentially one, but could be dissociated by a miracle. The same may be said

11 Cfr. *Opusc. Imperf. c. Iulian.*, V, 61: " *Donabit eam* [*scil. impeccantiam*] *veritas, ut sit certa securitas, sine qua non potest esse illa, cui non est aliquid addendum, iam plena nostra felicitas.*"

12 *Summa c. Gentiles*, IV, 92: " *Sed illi qui iam beati sunt, apprehendunt id, in quo vere beatitudo est, sub ratione beatitudinis et ultimi finis; alias in hoc non acquiesceret appetitus et per consequens non es-*

sent beati. Quicunque igitur beati sunt, voluntatem deflectere non possunt ab eo, in quo est vera beatitudo: non possunt igitur perversam voluntatem habere."

13 Cfr. St. Gregory the Great, *Moral.*, V, 27: " *Angelica natura in semetipsa mutabilis est, quam mutabilitatem vincit per hoc, quod ei qui semper idem est, vinculis amoris colligatur.*"

of the beatific vision and sorrow: these, too, are naturally
but not metaphysically incompatible.

3. THE OBJECT OF THE BEATIFIC VISION.—
What do the Blessed in Heaven actually behold
through the *lumen gloriae?* To answer this question we must distinguish between the Divine Essence and the things existing outside of it. The
Divine Essence itself is the object and source of
what is known as *beatitudo essentialis sive
primaria,* or *beatitudo aurea.* That secondary beatitude which the Scholastics term *accidentalis,* results from the contemplation of beautiful objects existing outside of the Divine Essence.
The essential beatitude of the Blessed consists
in an intuitive vision of the tri-une God with His
various attributes.[14]   To what objects the accidental beatitude of the Blessed extends cannot be
exactly determined.

a) From St. Paul's teaching in 1 Cor. XIII,
9 sqq. we know that the Blessed clearly behold
in Heaven whatever they embraced with theological faith on earth.   Faith is transformed into
knowledge.

It follows that the Blessed have a clear, though not an

---

14 Cfr. *Concil. Florent.,* 1439,
Denzinger-Bannwart, n. 693: " *Illorumque animas, qui post baptismum susceptum nullam omnino peccati maculam incurrerunt, illas etiam,
quae post contractam peccati maculam, vel in suis corporibus, vel eis-* *dem exutae corporibus, . . . sunt
purgatae, in caelum mox recipi et
intueri clare ipsum Deum trinum et
unum, sicuti est, pro meritorum tamen diversitate alium alio perfectius.*"

adequate, knowledge of all the theological mysteries (the Trinity, the Hypostatic Union of the two natures in Christ, the Holy Eucharist), and their mutual relations. *A fortiori* they must have a knowledge of the lesser mysteries of our holy religion, *e. g.* in what manner the Sacraments produce their effects, how the Holy Ghost operates in the Church and in the souls of the faithful, the nature of actual and sanctifying grace, the number of the Elect, predestination and reprobation, and many other things of which we on earth have at best only an inkling.

b) The beatific vision also involves a knowledge of the causal relations between God and all existing and possible creatures. This knowledge, however, is not shared equally by all the Blessed, but varies in clearness and depth in proportion to merit.

God is the cause of His creatures in a threefold respect: (1) as their pattern-exemplar (*causa exemplaris*), *i. e.* the model according to which they are fashioned; (2) as the efficient cause (*causa efficiens*) of both nature and the supernatural; and (3) as the final end and object (*causa finalis*) towards which all creatures consciously or unconsciously tend.[15] In all three of these respects the Blessed in Heaven perceive not only God's manifold relations to His creatures, but also the why and wherefore thereof, because knowledge of the Divine Essence necessarily includes knowledge of the divine ideas (though not of all), and the external glory of God, *i. e.* the admiration, love, and praise of His creatures, grows in proportion to their knowledge of His essence.

15 Cfr. Rom. XI, 36: "*Ex ipso, et per ipsum, et in ipso sunt omnia.*"

c) The beatitude enjoyed by the Blessed in Heaven is (*per accidens*) increased by their intimate association with the angels and saints.

The inhabitants of Heaven do not lead a solitary life, but are associated together in a mystic body called the Communion of Saints (*communio sanctorum*). They are members of the triumphant Church [16] and admiringly contemplate the angels in their hierarchical gradations as well as the various degrees of dignity and happiness manifested in their glorified fellowmen.[17] Their knowledge is not, however, limited to heavenly things, but extends to Purgatory and this earth, comprising especially those things which are closely related to the supernatural order in general and the position occupied therein by each heavenly denizen in particular. They devote special attention, of course, to whatever pertains to the worship and the intercession of the Saints. Bellarmine thinks that they derive their knowledge of these things from their official position in the celestial hierarchy rather than from a special revelation.

d) Various bonds connect the Blessed in Heaven with the scene of their labors, battles, temptations, and victories here below.

It was here that they acquired that more or less profound knowledge of science and art which is not lost but clarified, deepened, and ennobled in Heaven.[18] Here they

16 Cfr. Heb. II, 23.
17 Cfr. Lessius, *De Summo Bono,* II, 9, 61: "*Par enim est, ut civitatem suam et domum Patris sui et fratres suos et cives optime norint,* *et bonitatem Dei in singulis admirentur et laudent.*"
18 Cfr. 1 Cor. XIII, 10: "*Evacuabitur quod ex parte est.*"

still have relatives, friends, and descendants, in whom their former interest continues unabated, for Death does not destroy our earthly relations, but raises them to a higher sphere, in which the salvation of souls outweighs all other considerations. This knowledge the Elect can not obtain from personal observation, as they lack the organs of sense, but it is communicated to them by the Divine Logos, in whom they behold all things.[19]

4. THE "DOWRY" OF THE BLESSED.—By the dowry of the Blessed (*dotes beatorum*) the Scholastics understand those supernatural endowments by which the soul is distinguished in the beatific state.

a) Like the mystic marriage of the soul with Christ, the *dotes beatorum* must be conceived allegorically. As a dowry is not the matrimonial bond, but something which precedes marriage; so the dowry that Christ bestows on His mystic spouse is a habit which precedes the beatific vision and renders it more enjoyable.[20] The dowry of the Blessed is, however, purely accidental, and must not be confounded with the essence of the beatific vision, which consists in the intuitive knowledge of God.[21]

b) The gifts that constitute the dowry of the Blessed are partly of the body and partly of the soul. The dowry of the body is identical with the properties which we shall describe in Part II, Ch. II, Sect. 3. The dowry of the soul consists of the three gifts of contemplation,

---

19 Cfr. St. Thomas, *Summa c. Gentiles*, III, 50 — On the relations of the Elect to the objects of the beatific vision the student may consult Franzelin, *De Deo Uno*, thes. 18, Rome 1888.

20 Cfr. St. Thomas, *Comment. in Sent.*, IV, dist. 49, qu. 4, art. 2.

21 Cfr. St. Thomas, *Summa Theol., Supplement.*, qu. 95, art. 2.

possession, and fruition. Contemplation (*visio*) corresponds to faith, possession (*comprehensio*), to hope, fruition (*fruitio*), to charity. All three converge in the light of glory, which dispels the obscurity of faith, insures the eternal possession of God, and guarantees the enjoyment of His love.[22]

22 St. Thomas rejects the parallel drawn by some writers between the dowry of the Blessed and the three principal faculties of the soul. He says: "... *quia irascibilis et concupiscibilis non sunt in parte intellectiva, sed in parte sensitiva, dotes autem animae ponuntur in ipsa mente.*" (*Supplement.*, qu. 95, art. 5).— The question whether the soul of Christ possesses the *dotes beatorum* he answers as follows: "*Vel omnino non convenit Christo ratio dotis vel non ita proprie, sicut aliis sanctis; ea tamen, quae dotes dicuntur, excellentissime ei conveniunt.*" (*Ibid.*, art. 3). Of the angels he adds (*ibid.*, art. 4): "*Exigitur enim inter sponsum et sponsam naturae conformitas, ut scil. sint eiusdem speciei. Hoc autem modo homines cum Christo conveniunt, inquantum naturam humanam assumpsit. . . . Angelis autem non est conformis secundum unitatem speciei neque secundum naturam divinam neque secundum humanam, et ideo ratio dotis non ita proprie convenit angelis sicut hominibus.*"— The Scholastic doctrine of the *dotes beatorum* is of no special importance.

SECTION 2

THE PROPERTIES OF HEAVEN

Heaven is supernatural and eternal, and has various degrees of happiness for the Blessed, corresponding to the higher or lower measure of grace with which each is endowed and the intimacy of his union with God.[1]

1. ETERNITY OF HEAVEN.—The eternity of Heaven was in olden times denied by the Origenists. Benedict XII defined it as an article of faith: "This same vision and fruition . . . continues and will continue till the final judgment, and thenceforward forever." [2] The dogma is as old as Christianity, for the Apostles' Creed says: "I believe . . . in life everlasting."

a) Sacred Scripture employs many beautiful figures to illustrate the perpetuity of Heaven. Thus it compares Heaven to "a treasure which faileth not," which "no thief approacheth, nor moth corrupteth;" [3] a reception "into everlast-

1 On the supernatural character of the beatific vision see Pohle-Preuss, *God: His Knowability, Essence, and Attributes,* pp. 80 sqq.

2 Cfr. the Bull *" Benedictus,"* A. D. 1336: *" Eadem visio et fruitio . . . continuata existit et conti-* *nuabitur usque ad finale iudicium, et tunc usque in sempiternum."* (Denzinger-Bannwart, n. 531).

3 Luke XII, 33: *". . . thesaurum non deficientem in caelis: quo fur non appropriat, neque tinea corrumpit."*

39

ing dwellings;" [4] "a never fading crown of glory;" [5] an "everlasting kingdom." [6] St. John frequently refers to the abode of the Blessed as "eternal life." [7]

b) The Fathers conceived Heaven as unending. Heaven must be everlasting, says St. Augustine, because no happiness could be perfect that would be overshadowed by the fear of a possible cessation or loss.[8] St. Thomas defines eternity as an intrinsic and essential quality without which Heaven would not be Heaven. The opinion of some of the later Scotists that eternity is an accidental quality of beatitude, is untenable.

2. VARIOUS DEGREES OF HAPPINESS AMONG THE BLESSED.—The ancient heretic Jovinian held that virtues and vices, merits and demerits, rewards and punishments are all alike. Luther, in accordance with his false theory of justification, contended that glory as well as grace are absolutely equal in all men and do not admit of degrees. The Catholic Church, on the contrary, holds as an article of faith that there are among the Blessed various degrees of happiness, in propor-

---

[4] Luke XVI, 9: " *Facite vobis amicos de mammona iniquitatis: ut, quum defeceritis, recipiant vos in aeterna tabernacula.*"

[5] 1 Pet. V, 4: " *Quum apparuerit princeps pastorum, percipietis immarcescibilem gloriae coronam.*"

[6] 2 Pet. I, 11: " *aeternum regnum Domini.*"

[7] *Vita aeterna*, ζωὴ αἰώνιος.

[8] *De Civ. Dei*, XII, 20: " *Quid enim illâ beatitudine falsius atque fallacius, ubi nos futuros miseros aut in tantâ veritatis luce nesciamus aut in summâ felicitatis arce timeamus?* . . . *Atque ita spes nostrae infelicitatis est felix et felicitatis infelix.*"

tion to merit. "One is more perfect than the other according to the different merits of each," says *e. g.* the *Decretum Unionis* of Florence.[9]

a) This teaching agrees perfectly with Sacred Scripture. Our Lord Himself intimates that there are various degrees of happiness among the Elect, when He says: "In my Father's house there are many mansions."[10] St. Paul expressly declares: "Each shall receive his own reward according to his own toil."[11] And: "He who soweth sparingly, shall also reap sparingly, and he who soweth in blessings, shall also reap blessings."[12] And again: "The glory of the heavenly is different from that of the earthly. There is the glory of the sun, and the glory of the moon, and the glory of the stars; for star differeth from star in glory. And so it is with the resurrection of the dead."[13]

The Fathers express themselves in similar terms. St. Polycarp bravely assures his heathen judge: "The more I suffer, the greater will be my reward."[14] St. Ignatius

---

9 ". . . *pro meritorum tamen diversitate alium alio perfectius.*" (Denzinger-Bannwart, n. 693).

10 John XIV, 2: "*In domo Patris mei mansiones multae sunt.*"

11 1 Cor. III, 8: "*Unusquisque autem propriam mercedem accipiet secundum suum laborem.*"

12 2 Cor. IX, 6: "*Qui parce seminat, parce et metet: et qui seminat in benedictionibus, de benedictionibus et metet.*"

13 1 Cor. XV, 41 sq.: "*Alia claritas solis, alia claritas lunae, et alia claritas stellarum. Stella enim a stella differt in claritate: sic et resurrectio mortuorum.*"—Cfr. Al. Schäfer, *Erklärung der beiden Briefe an die Korinther*, pp. 228 sqq., Münster 1903; J. MacRory, *The Epistles of St. Paul to the Corinthians*, P. I, pp. 245 sq., Dublin 1915.

14 *Martyrium S. Polycarpi*, 40.

of Antioch writes: "The greater the toil, the greater the gain." [15] Tertullian says: "How is it that there are many mansions in the Father's house, if not for the variety of merits? How does star differ from star in glory, if not for the diversity of rays?" [16] St. Jerome argues against Jovinian: "If there is no difference in merits, if virgins do not differ from married women, if the easier works of piety are equally meritorious with the constancy of the martyrs, it is vain to strive for perfection," and proceeds to show how absurd it is to suppose that a death-bed repentance puts the life-long sinner on a level with the Apostles. [17]

The objection that inequality of glory in Heaven would provoke envy and jealousy among the Blessed, is refuted by St. Augustine as follows: "There will be no envy on account of unequal glory, because one love will govern all." [18] According to St. Thomas the measure of glory enjoyed by each is gauged by the strength of the love he has for God: "That intellect which has more of the light of glory will see God the more perfectly; and he will have a fuller participation of the light of glory who has more of charity, because where there is greater charity, there is a more ardent desire; . . . hence he who possesses the greater charity, will see God the more perfectly." [19]

[15] *Ad Polycarp.*, I, 3: ὅπου πλείων κόπος, πολὺ κέρδος.

[16] *Scorpiace*, 6: "*Quomodo multae mansiones apud Patrem, si non pro varietate meritorum? Quomodo et stella a stella distabit in gloria, nisi pro diversitate radiorum?*"

[17] *Contra Iovin.*, II, 34: "*Si nulla meritorum diversitas, si nihil distet inter virgines et mulieres coniugatas, si aequalis meriti sint leviora virtutum opera et martyrum constantia, vanum erit perfectionis studium, taediosus omnino erit virtutum labor, omnes a perfectione retrahentur. Quid perseverant virgines? Quid laborant viduae? Cur maritatae se continent? Peccemus omnes, et post poenitentiam idem erimus quod Apostoli sunt.*"

[18] *Tract. in Ioa.*, 67, 3: "*Non erit aliqua invidia imparis claritatis, quoniam regnabit in omnibus unitas caritatis.*"

[19] *Summa Theol.*, 1a, qu. 12, art. 6: "*Intellectus plus participans de*

b) The inequality of heavenly glory has given rise to the Scholastic doctrine of *aureolae, i. e.* special marks of success attaching to those who have won conspicuous victories over the three arch-enemies of man, the world, the flesh, and the devil.[20]

The aureola of the virgin marks a heroic victory over the flesh;[21] that of the martyr, over the world;[22] that of the doctor, over the devil, who is the father of lies.[23] These marks must be something real, immanent in the soul, and may be conceived as an internal joy over the victory won. What some theologians say of the external visibility of these crowns of glory, or their color, is pure conjecture.

READINGS:— *Lessius, *De Summo Bono et Aeterna Beatitudine Hominis*, Antwerp 1616 (ed. Hurter, 1869).— Suarez, *De Fine Ultimo.*—* Bellarmine, *De Sanctorum Beatitudine.*— Schnütgen, *Die Visio Beatifica*, Würzburg 1867.— A Krawutzcky, *De Visione Beatifica Comment. Histor.*, Breslau 1868.— Kirschkamp, *Gnade und Glorie in ihrem inneren Zusammenhang*, Würzburg 1878.— *Bautz, *Der Himmel, spekulativ dargestellt*, Mayence 1881.— *Franzelin, *De Deo Uno*, thes. 14–19, Rome 1888.— F. Boudreaux, S.J., *Die Seligkeit des Himmels*, Kevelaer 1898.— Scheeben, *Die Mysterien des Christentums*, 3rd ed., pp. 583 sqq., Freiburg 1912. — E. Méric, *Les Élus se reconnaîtront au Ciel*, Paris 1881.— Blot, S.J., *Das Wiedererkennen im Jenseits*, 10th ed., Mayence

---

lumine gloriae perfectius Deum videbit. Plus autem participabit de lumine gloriae, qui plus habet de caritate, quia ubi est maior caritas, ibi est maius desiderium. . . . Unde qui plus habebit de caritate, perfectius Deum videbit."

20 Cfr. St. Thomas, *Summa Theol., Supplement.*, qu. 95, art. 1: "*Au-*

reola est aliquid aureae [beatitudini essentiali] superadditum, i. e. quoddam gaudium de operibus a se factis, quae habent rationem victoriae excellentis."

21 Apoc. XIV, 3.
22 Cfr. Matth. V, 11 sq.
23 Cfr. Dan. XII, 3.

1900.— G. Gietmann, S.J., art. "Nimbus," in Vol. XI of the *Catholic Encyclopedia.*— Jos. Hontheim, S.J., art. "Heaven," *ibid.,* Vol. VII.

CHAPTER IV

HELL

SECTION 1

THE EXISTENCE OF HELL

1. DEFINITION.—Our English word "Hell" comes from the Anglo-Saxon *hel*, which originally signified "a hidden place." [1] According to present-day usage Hell means the abode of evil spirits and the place or state of punishment of the wicked after death. The Hebrew term *sheol* is sometimes used in the same sense, though its proper meaning is "cave," "nether world," or "abode of the departed." The Latin *infernus* (Greek, ᾅδης) more definitely signifies the place where the wicked are tormented. The Hebrew name for this place is *gehenna*, which originally meant "valley of the Hinnom." This valley was near Jerusalem and once belonged to the sons of Hinnom (Ennom). Later it became the scene of cruel sacrifices to Moloch and finally served as a garbage dump. [2] The term *gehenna* in the sense

---

1 See the Oxford *New English Dictionary*, Vol. V, *s. v.*   2 Cfr. 4 Kings XXIII, 10; Jer. VII, 31; XIX, 6.

of *infernus* was in common use among the Jews at the time of our Lord.[3]

Besides these more or less technical terms, Holy Scripture employs a number of metaphorical expressions to designate the abode of the damned, *e. g.,* " exterior darkness," accompanied by "weeping and gnashing of teeth;"[4] "everlasting fire;"[5] "the second death,"[6] etc. Though all these phrases, with the exception of the last, may connote a place, the emphasis is upon the *state* of eternal damnation and torment. Very truly, therefore, has it been said that the damned carry Hell around with them.

2. THE EXISTENCE OF HELL PROVED FROM SACRED SCRIPTURE AND TRADITION.—The existence of Hell was denied by the Jewish sect of the Sadducees, by the followers of the Gnostic heretic Valentinus, and, generally, by unbelievers of all ages. The Catholic Church, on the contrary, has repeatedly and solemnly defined that "the wicked [will receive] eternal punishment together with the devil."[7]

a) Sacred Scripture inculcates this truth so frequently and unmistakably that it has been justly said that no other Catholic dogma has such a solid Biblical basis. St. Jude designates Hell as

---

3 Cfr. Matth. V, 22, 29; Mark IX, 46; Luke XII, 5.

4 *Tenebrae exteriores,* σκότος ἐξώτερον. (Matth. VIII, 12).

5 Matth. XXV, 41; Mark IX, 42.

6 *V. supra,* p. 5.

7 *Conc. Lat. IV, Cap.* "*Firmiter*": "*Illi [scil. mali] cum diabolo poenam perpetuam et isti [scil. boni] cum Christo gloriam sempiternam [recipient]."* (Denzinger-Bannwart, n. 429).

"the punishment of eternal fire." [8]   St. Paul calls
it "eternal punishment in destruction." [9]   Our
Lord Himself describes it as an "unquenchable
fire," a place "where the worm dieth not and the
fire is not extinguished," [10] a "furnace of fire," [11]
etc.   St. John in the Apocalypse refers to Hell as
"a pool burning with fire and brimstone." [12]
Many other texts could be cited, but it is unneces-
sary to multiply proofs in view of our Lord's own
declaration that the wicked will be cast into an
"everlasting fire, which was prepared for the devil
and his angels." [13]

b) The Fathers faithfully echo this teaching
of Scripture.   Thus St. Ignatius of Antioch
writes to the Ephesians: "Do not err, my brethren; . . . if a man by false teaching corrupt the
faith of God, for the sake of which Jesus Christ
was crucified, such a one shall go in his foulness
to the unquenchable fire,[14] as also shall he who lis-
tens to him." [15]   Not content with testifying to
the teaching of Scripture on the subject, the Fathers proved it from reason.   Thus they argue
that God in His justice cannot possibly allow crim-

8 Jude 7: " *ignis aeterni poenam.*"
9 2 Thess. I, 9: " *Qui poenas da-*
bunt in interitu aeternas a facie
Domini. . . ."
10 Mark IX, 43: " *Ubi vermis*
eorum non moritur, et ignis non
extinguitur."
11 Matth. XIII, 42: " *Et mittent*
eos in caminum ignis . . ."
12 Apoc. XXI, 8: ". . . *pars il-*
lorum erit in stagno ardenti igne
et sulphure: quod est mors secunda."
— For other expressions see No. 1,
supra.
13 Matth. XXV, 41: " *Discedite*
a me maledicti in ignem aeternum,
qui paratus est diabolo et angelis
suis."
14 εἰς τὸ πῦρ τὸ ἄσβεστον.
15 *Ad Eph.,* XVI, 2.

inals to go unpunished. "I will briefly reply," says St. Justin Martyr, "that if the matter be not thus, either there is no God, or if there is, He does not concern Himself with men, virtue and vice mean nothing, and they who transgress important laws are unjustly punished by the lawgivers." [16]   St. Chrysostom writes: "All of us,— Greeks and Jews, heretics and Christians,—acknowledge that God is just. Now many who sinned have passed away without being punished, while many others, who led virtuous lives, did not die until they had suffered innumerable tribulations.   If God is just, how will He reward the latter and punish the former, unless there be a Hell and a Resurrection?" [17]

c) A cogent philosophical argument for the existence of Hell can be drawn from the consensus of mankind that there must be a place where criminals receive their just punishment in the next world. This belief is so general, so definite, and so clearly demanded by reason that it must be true.

Society and the moral order could not exist without belief in Hell, and it is probably on this account that all nations have clung to this belief despite its terrors. Those individuals who deny the existence of Hell are mostly atheists or libertines, distinguished neither for learning nor purity of life. Wherever conscience is allowed to speak, it voices the firm conviction that God will punish the wicked and reward the just in the world

16 *Apol.*, II, n. 9.   — Other Patristic testimonies *infra.*
17 *Hom. in Ep. ad Phil.*, 6, n. 6.   Sect. 3.

beyond. St. Chrysostom aptly observes: " If those who argue against Hell would embrace virtue, they would soon be convinced of its existence." [18]

2. THE LOCATION OF HELL.—The Fathers and Scholastics believed Hell to be somewhere under the earth or near its centre, which latter view is immortalized in Dante's Inferno.[19] This ancient belief was based on such Biblical passages as Numb. XVI, 31 sqq.: "Immediately as he had made an end of speaking, the earth broke asunder under their feet, and opening her mouth, devoured them with their tents and all their substance, and they went down alive into hell." Ps. LIV, 16: "Let death come upon them, and let them go down alive into hell." Isaias V, 14: "Therefore hath hell . . . opened her mouth, and their strong ones . . . shall go down into it." Our Lord Jesus Christ Himself "descended into hell."[20]

a) But these texts no more prove that Hell is beneath or in the earth than the ancient conception of Heaven as " above " proves that the abode of the Blessed is located somewhere beyond the firmament. The ancients had a

18 *Hom. in Ep. ad Rom.*, 31, n. 4.— The argument from reason in St. Thomas, *Summa c. Gent.*, III, 140; *Summa Theol.*, 1a 2ae, qu. 87, art. 1.— Cfr. H. Lüken, *Die Traditionen des Menschengeschlechtes*, 2nd ed., pp. 410 sqq., Münster 1869.
19 Cfr. Patruzzi, *De Sede Inferni in Terra Quaerenda*, Venice 1763.

20 Cfr. Pohle-Preuss, *Soteriology*, p. 91.— Other Patristic utterances in Lessius, *De Perfect. Moribusque Divinis*, XIII, 24.— The question regarding the probable location of Hell is treated at length by Bautz, *Die Hölle, im Anschluss an die Scholastik*, 2nd ed., pp. 28 sqq., Mayence 1905.

geocentric conception of the universe, which found its scientific expression in the Ptolemaic system. To them the earth was the centre of the universe, surrounded in great circles, called deferents, by the revolving centers of smaller circles, called epicycles, on whose circumferences the planets were supposed to move. Beyond the last and highest sphere was an imaginary region of light, the empyreum, to which fire and other tenuous bodies were believed to tend as to their natural goal. This conception of the universe led the Scholastics to locate Heaven in the empyreum and Hell in the centre of the earth, with Purgatory and the Limbo somewhere in the outer strata of our planet. Those who, like Cosmas Indicopleustes,[21] conceived the earth as a rectangular plane encircled by steep walls, placed Hell underneath this plane.

b) It is easy to ridicule these naïve ideas from the advanced standpoint of modern science, as Draper and Flammarion have done. But no sane philosopher will argue that Hell does not exist because " there is no place for it in the heliocentric system." We readily admit that modern astronomy has corrected many erroneous notions and that the progress of geography and physics has exercised a wholesome influence on Eschatology. To-day " above " and " below " are recognized as purely relative terms, and we know that the heavens constantly change their position towards us as the earth revolves around its own axis and around the sun. Holy Scripture and the Fathers speak the language of the common people, and such phrases as take the geocentric system for granted, must not be interpreted literally. The unfortunate Galileo case is a warning to theolo-

21 Topographia Christiana, 1. II. (On this writer and his Christian Topography cfr. Bardenhewer-Sha-han, Patrology, pp. 555 sq., St. Louis 1908).

gians. The Church has never defined that Hell is a *place*, though the dogma of the Resurrection seems to entail this conclusion. Still less has she defined *where* Hell is. That is a question lying entirely outside the sphere of dogma. St. Gregory the Great says: "I dare not define anything on this subject, for some believed Hell to be situated somewhere within the earth, whereas others look for it under the earth." [22] In point of fact we know nothing at all about it, and rather than pry into the unknowable, we ought to heed the warning of St. Chrysostom: "Do not inquire where Hell is, but how to escape it." [23]

---

[22] *Dial.*, IV, 42: "*De hac re temere definire nihil audeo. Nonnulli namque in quadam terrarum parte infernum esse putaverunt, alii vero hunc sub terra esse aestimant.*" (Migne, *P. L.*, LXXVII, 400).

[23] *Hom. in Ep. ad Rom.*, 31, n. 5 (Migne, *P. G.*, LX, 674).

SECTION 2

NATURE OF THE PUNISHMENT

Though the Church has defined nothing with regard to the nature of the punishment which the wicked are compelled to suffer in Hell, theologians usually describe it as partly privative and partly positive.

Its most dreadful element is undoubtedly the loss of the beatific vision. To this (*poena damni*) are added certain positive torments (*poena sensus*).

The twofold punishment of the wicked, according to St. Thomas, corresponds to the twofold nature of sin, which is both a turning away from God (*aversio a Deo*) and an inordinate turning towards the creature (*conversio ad creaturam*). "Punishment," he says, "is proportionate to sin. Now sin comprises two things. First, there is the turning away from the immutable good, which is infinite, and therefore, in this respect, sin is infinite. Secondly, there is the inordinate turning to mutable good. In this respect sin is finite, both because the mutable good itself is finite, and because the movement of turning towards it is finite, since the acts of a creature cannot be infinite. Accordingly, in so far as sin consists in turning away from God, its corresponding punishment is the pain of loss, which also is infinite, because it is the loss of the infinite good, *i. e.* God. But in so far as sin turns inordinately [to the mutable good], its corresponding punishment is the pain of sense, which also is finite."[1]

I. THE PAIN OF LOSS (POENA DAMNI).— Damnation consists essentially in a realization on the part of the creature of the fact that through its own fault it has lost the greatest of all goods and missed the very purpose of its existence, and thereby its natural destiny. This knowledge causes a feeling of unhappiness akin to desperation, which is the exact counterpart of the beatitude of Heaven. The *poena damni* is expressed in the words, "Depart from me, ye cursed!" whereas the *poena sensus* is indicated in the phrase, "into eternal fire."[2] There are other Scriptural texts that confirm this doctrine. Luke

[1] *Summa Theol.*, 1a 2ae, qu. 87, art. 4: "*Poena proportionatur peccato. In peccato autem duo sunt: quorum unum est aversio ab incommutabili bono, quod est infinitum, unde ex hac parte peccatum est infinitum; aliud quod est in peccato est inordinata conversio ad commutabile bonum; et ex hac parte peccatum est finitum, tum quia ipsum bonum commutabile est finitum, tum etiam quia ipsa conversio est finita; non enim possunt esse actus creaturae infiniti. Ex parte igitur aversionis respondet peccato poena damni, quae etiam est infinita; est enim amissio infiniti boni, scilicet Dei. Ex parte autem inordinatae conversionis respondet ei poena sensus, quae etiam est finita.*"

[2] *V. infra*, No. 2.

XIV, 24: "But I say unto you that none of those men that were invited, shall taste of my supper." [3] In the parable of the Master of the house, Luke XIII, 27 sq., the Lord says: "I know you not, whence you are: depart from me, all ye workers of iniquity. There shall be weeping and gnashing of teeth, when you shall see Abraham and Isaac and Jacob, and all the prophets, in the kingdom of God, and you yourselves thrust out." [4]

The Fathers unanimously confirm the teaching of Scripture. St. John Chrysostom describes the pain of loss, in contradistinction to the pain of sense, as follows: "The fire of Hell is insupportable—who does not know it?—and its torments are awful. But if you were to heap a thousand hell-fires one on top of the other, it would be as nothing compared to the punishment [that consists in] being excluded from the beatific glory of Heaven, hated by Christ, and compelled to hear Him say, 'I know thee not.'" [5]

It is difficult, nay impossible, to write a psychology of the damned. This much, however, is certain: the reprobates in Hell are beyond redemption and sanctifying grace in their souls is replaced by a fierce hatred of Almighty God.

3 Luke XIV, 24: "*Dico autem vobis, quod nemo virorum illorum, qui vocati sunt, gustabit coenam meam.*"

4 Luke XIII, 27 sq.: "*Nescio vos, unde sitis: discedite a me omnes operarii iniquitatis. Ibi erit fletus et stridor dentium: quum videritis Abraham et Isaac et Iacob et omnes prophetas in regno Dei, vos autem expelli foras.*"

5 *Hom. in Matth.*, 23, n. 8.

Schell [6] has protested against the " rigorism " which asserts that the will of the wicked after death is suddenly set against God and that their previous half-hearted love of, or indifference towards Him, becomes transformed into " satanic malice." The germs of moral good which a soul takes with it into the next world, he argues, cannot be lost, since God destroys no good thing. This doubtful principle led Schell to conclusions closely akin to those of Hirscher.[7] His teaching was violently assailed by Father J. Stufler, S. J.[8] Professor F. X. Kiefl defended Schell and interpreted his words more mildly. It is undeniable, however, because of the essential distinction existing between the *status viae* and the *status termini,* that when the damned enter Hell, where grace ceases and conversion becomes impossible, they are smitten with great confusion of spirit and a corresponding sentiment of impenitence. Being permanently deprived of grace makes them enemies of God. It is not necessary to conceive this state as a sort of confirmed " Satanism." No doubt there are degrees of malice and impenitence in Hell. But all the damned hate God more or less because He is no longer their friend. Herein lies the dreadfulness of eternal punishment. The natural will, being a gift of God, remains good; but it no longer wills that which is good. It wills the bad, or if it wills the good, wills it with a wrong intention. St. Thomas explains the reason as follows: " The damned are absolutely turned away from the final end of the rightly directed will. The will cannot be good except it be ordered to that end, so that, even if [the damned] willed something good, they would not will it in the right way, *i. e.* so

6 *Dogmatik,* Vol. II, Part II, pp. 745 sqq.

7 *V. supra,* p. 15.

8 *Die Heiligkeit Gottes und der ewige Tod,* Innsbruck 1904.

that their will might be called good."[9] Though such an exercise of the will is sinful, it entails no demerit, because the damned are in the *status termini*.[10] Hence the damned by the sins which they commit in Hell do not merit an increase of the *poena damni* or of the torments which constitute the *poena sensus*. This is the common teaching of Catholic theologians, based on the wisdom and justice of God.[11]

2. THE PAIN OR PUNISHMENT OF SENSE (POENA SENSUS).—"Pain of sense" in Catholic theology means a pain which is caused by a sensible medium, regardless of whether it is felt by the senses or not.[12] The external medium through which the positive punishments of Hell are inflicted is called by Sacred Scripture fire (*ignis*, πῦρ). Must this term be taken literally or may it be interpreted in a metaphorical sense?

" The worm that dieth not "[13] is undoubtedly a figure of speech, signifying the pangs of conscience, and hence there is no intrinsic reason why the word " fire " might not signify mental anguish, as Origen, Ambrose Catharinus,[14] Möhler,[15] and others have maintained. The

9 *Comment. in Sent.*, IV, dist. 50, qu. 2, art. 1: " *Et hoc ideo, quia sunt perfecte aversi a fine ultimo rectae voluntatis. Nec aliqua voluntas potest esse bona nisi per ordinem ad finem praedictum, unde etiam si aliquid bonum velint, non tamen bene bonum volunt illud, ut ex hoc voluntas eorum bona dici possit.*"
10 *V.* Ch. I, Thesis III, p. 13.
11 Cfr. Chr. Pesch, S.J., *Theo-*logische Zeitfragen, 2te Folge; pp. 83 sqq., Freiburg 1901; J. Lehner, *Der Willenszustand des Sünders nach dem Tode*, Vienna 1906.
12 Cfr. Suarez, *De Angelis*, VIII, 12.
13 Mark IX, 43.
14 *Opuscula*, ed. Lugdun., 1542, pp. 145 sqq.
15 *Neue Untersuchungen*, 5th ed., p. 318, Ratisbon 1890.

Church has never issued a dogmatic definition on the subject. Hence we are not dealing with an article of faith nor even with a *sententia fidei proxima.* However, as the literal interpretation is favored by the great majority of Fathers and Scholastics, it may be regarded as " *sententia certa.*"

There must be some external medium or agent —(whether solid, fluid or gaseous, or in some state transcending the laws of nature)—by which the wicked are tormented, and the nature of which is absolutely unknown to us. In taking this position we oppose the naïve realism of those who regard Hell as literally a gigantic "furnace" or an active volcano.

a) In trying to ascertain the nature of the infernal fire, the first thing that strikes us is that, though it is physical and real, it cannot be material.

α) Neither in its nature nor in its properties, neither in its beneficent nor in its malign effects, is the fire of Hell identical with, or even similar to, the material fire of nature.

Sacred Scripture speaks of Hell as a " furnace of fire," a " pool of fire and brimstone," an " external darkness in which there is howling and gnashing of teeth," an " eternal fire " prepared for the devil and his angels from the beginning.[16] Now the devil and his angels (the demons), being pure spirits, cannot be affected by material substances such as fire and brimstone, heat and darkness, because they possess neither senses nor sen-

16 *V. supra,* Sect. 1.

sitive faculties. The same is true of the souls of the wicked during their disembodied state, i. e. before the Resurrection of the flesh.

This fact was clearly perceived by the Fathers. Lactantius says: " The nature of that everlasting fire is different from this fire of ours, which we use for the necessary purposes of life, and which ceases to burn unless it be sustained by the fuel of some material. But that divine fire always lives by itself, and burns without nourishment; nor has it any smoke mixed with it, but it is pure and liquid and fluid, after the manner of water." [17] St. Ephraem [18] and St. Basil [19] declare that the fire of Hell causes darkness and incessantly torments its victims, without however destroying them. St. Ambrose writes: " Therefore it is neither a gnashing of the bodily teeth, nor a perpetual bodily fire, nor a bodily worm." [20] St. Augustine says that the fire of Hell, while it bears some resemblance to our material fire, is not identical with it.[21] St. John of Damascus teaches: " The devil and his angels and his man, i. e. Antichrist, as well as all other impious and wicked men, will be thrust into eternal fire, [which is] not a material fire like ours, but of a quality known to God." [22]

β) A few Catholic theologians (Henry of Ghent, Toletus, Tanner, Lessius, and Fr. Schmid [23]) conceive the

---

[17] De Div. Inst., VII, 21.
[18] Serm. Exeget., Opera Syriace et Latine, Vol. II, p. 354.
[19] In Psal., 28, 7, n. 6.
[20] In Lucam, VII. n. 204: " Ergo neque est corporalium stridor aliquis dentium neque ignis aliquis perpetuus flammarum corporalium neque vermis est corporalis."
[21] De Genesi ad Literam, XII, 32,

61: " Non esse corporalia, sed similia corporalibus, quibus animae corporibus exutae afficiantur."
[22] οὐχ ὑλικόν, οἷον τὸ παρ' ἡμῖν. ἀλλ' οἷον ἂν εἰδείη ὁ Θεός. (De Fide Orthodoxa, IV, 27).— Some of the Fathers explain the term "eternal fire" metaphorically; cfr. Pesch, Praelect. Dogmat., Vol. IX, 2nd ed., pp. 322 sq.
[23] Quaestiones Selectae, pp. 145 sqq., Paderborn 1891.

action of the infernal fire upon the demons and the souls
of the wicked as that of a material upon an immaterial
substance.[24] Opposed to this theory is the fact that pure
spirits as well as disembodied souls are utterly devoid of
sense perception. But could not God make them feel
sensual pain by a miracle? That depends on the
answer to another question, *viz.:* Is there an intrinsic
contradiction involved in the assertion that pure spirits
can be affected by a material substance? Neither philosophy nor Revelation gives a definite answer to this
question. The existing uncertainty has led other theologians to devise a more plausible theory. They regard
the effect of the fire of Hell as purely spiritual, holding
that the constant presence of fire, which is a material
element, occupies the intellect of the damned in a dis-
agreeable manner and fills the will with sadness
and aversion,[25] or the fact of their being locally and in-
separably bound up with this lowly element [26] hinders the
free activity of the spirit and thus causes internal anguish
(*per modum detentionis*). The souls of the lost before
the Resurrection, says St. Thomas, "shall suffer from
corporeal fire by a sort of constriction (*alligatio*). For
spirits can be tied to bodies, either as their form, as the
soul is tied to the human body to give it life; or without
being the body's form, as magicians by diabolic power
tie spirits to images.[27] Much more by divine power may
spirits under damnation be tied to corporeal fire; and it
is an affliction to them to know that they are tied to the
meanest creatures for punishment." [28] This opinion is

24 Cfr. Lessius, *De Div. Perf.*,
XIII, 30: "*Si ignis naturaliter per
suum calorem potest affligere spiritum
hominis mediante corpore, cur idem
ignis ut instrumentum Dei non poterit affligere eundem spiritum sine*

ullo corpore medio?"
25 Cfr. St. Thomas, *Summa Theol.*,
Supplement., qu. 70, art. 3.
26 Cfr. 2 Pet. II, 4; Jude 6.
27 See Rickaby's note on this passage in *God and His Creatures*, p.
413, London 1905.

shared by the majority of Thomists. Suarez goes
so far as to say [29] that the effect of hell-fire is purely
spiritual, disfiguring the demons and the disembodied
souls of the lost in a manner analogous to that in which
sanctifying grace beautifies the angels and saints. This
theory, though it correctly emphasizes the mysterious nature of the fire, reduces it to the level of an intangible
metaphor.

One thing has been made certain by the subtle debates
of the Schoolmen, namely, that the fire of Hell cannot be
identical with material fire, but must be something at the
same time physical and supra-physical, a punishment in-
vented by an avenging God, of which we know nothing
except that it exists and torments the damned.

b) What we have so far said applies principally to the demons, who are pure spirits; but it
is applicable also to the souls of the wicked before the Resurrection.

These souls, it is true, do not lose their sensitive faculties when they leave the body. But they become incapable
of sense perception for lack of adequate organs (brain
and nervous system). "Incorporeal subsistent spirits,"
says St. Thomas, "have no organs of sense nor the use
of sensory powers." [30] It is different after the Resurrection, when the souls are reunited with their bodies.
"Whatever may be said of the fire which torments the
disembodied souls," adds the Angelic Doctor, "the fire
that torments the bodies of the damned after the Res-

28 *Summa Contra Gent.*, IV, 90;
cfr. *De Veritate*, qu. 26, art. 1.
29 *De Angelis*, VIII, 14.
30 " *Substantiae incorporeae organa*
sensuum non habent neque potentiis
sensitivis utuntur." (*Summa contra*
Gent., IV, 90).

urrection must be regarded as corporeal, because a pain
is not adapted to the body unless it is a bodily pain." [31]
Nevertheless, the theory we have set forth is not
free from difficulties. It implies two strange corollaries,
viz.: (1) that the pains of sense which the souls of the
lost suffer in Hell differ before and after the Resurrection; and (2) that the souls of wicked men throughout eternity suffer more intensely than the demons, for
whom the everlasting fire was originally prepared. For
if that fire be qualitatively the same for the demons and
the souls of wicked men, it must cause the same kind of
pain to both. True, the body, too, is affected; but this
bodily pain need not be conceived as a real burning; it
may be something entirely *sui generis*. We can obtain no
certain knowledge in the matter, though the possibility of
a real burning is undeniable. However, if we consider
that the assumption of a material fire, or a fire analogous
to the material, does not sufficiently account for either
the quantitative inequality of the torments inflicted or their
qualitative adaptability to the different kinds of sins to
be punished, we shall be confirmed in the conviction that
the fire of Hell in no wise resembles the material fire of
nature.[32]

[31] " *Quidquid dicatur de igne, qui
animas separatas cruciat, de igne
tamen, quo cruciabuntur corpora
damnatorum post resurrectionem,
oportet dicere, quod sit corporeus,
quia corpori non potest convenienter
adaptari poena, nisi sit corporea."*
(*Summa Theol., Supplement.*, qu. 79,
art. 5).

[32] Fr. Joseph Rickaby, S. J., says
in a recent brochure (*Everlasting
Punishment*, pp. 7-11, London 1916):
" The fire of hell is real fire:
that is to say, the word *fire* is the
most proper and exact word which

human speech affords to tell us
what that terrible thing is. Everlasting fire ' is not a figurative expression; it occurs in a judicial sentence. Judges in passing sentence
do not use figurative language; not
in any figurative or metaphorical
sense shall you be ' hung by the neck
till you are dead.' At the same
time we have no exact and certain
knowledge of the precise nature of
the fire of hell. Is it exactly like
the fire of earth? But what exactly
is the fire of earth? What is combustion? Not till the end of the

But if this be true, why does Sacred Scripture call the mysterious medium of eternal punishment " fire "? Why not " water," or " snow," or " ether "? The answer is

eighteenth century was man able to reply, combustion is rapid combination with oxygen.' Our ancestors did not scientifically know what fire was. They thought it was a ' substance,' an ' element,' the lightest and in natural position the highest of the four elements, fire, air, water, and earth, out of which all bodies were composed. So then the fire of hell, if it really was fire, they thought must be a substance too. So it well may be, but we must speak cautiously. Modern science presents us with heat, fire, light, and electricity, and tells us that they are all so many, not substances or elements, but modes of motion affecting substance, whatever substance may be. They are most abundant things in nature: the fixed stars are all on fire; electricity is suspected of being a primary constituent of matter. We know much more about these things than our ancestors did: still we are in great perplexity over them, indeed our perplexities grow with our knowledge. Such is our ignorance of the fire of this world, matter though it be of our daily experience. Of a fire such as that in which angels and disembodied souls burn, happily we have no experience. And beyond teaching us that there is such a fire, real fire, Christian revelation does not go. It would be therefore extremely rash, beyond the existence (*an sit*) of such a fire, to pretend to lay down with certainty its nature, qualities, composition, and mode of action (*quid sit*). The Church does not do so. Her theologians echo St. Augustine's words: ' As to which fire, of what sort, and in what part

of the world or universe it is to be, I am of opinion that no man knows, unless haply some one to whom the Spirit of God has shown it.' (*Qui ignis cujusmodi et in qua mundi vel rerum parte futurus sit hominem scire arbitror neminem, nisi forte cui Spiritus divinus revelavit.— De Civitate Dei*, xx. 16). There is, however, a general consent of the faithful to regard it as a ' material ' fire, and though this be not absolutely of faith, still. it cannot be denied without incurring the theological note of ' rashness.' In accordance with this general consent I have described it as ' a material environment.' A further speculation: is this material environment itself on fire, or is it such that the soul chafing and struggling against that constraint —' the great net of slavery,' μέγα δουλείας γάγγαμον, to borrow a phrase of Æschylus — and, as St. Teresa says, ' continually tearing herself in pieces '— thereby sets herself on fire? The question is beyond our knowledge to answer. We are accustomed to pictures of flames, with souls in bodily shapes writhing in them, and in such sensible representations we must fain acquiesce as being the best way to bring home to imagination the reality of hell-fire. God knows His own justice, which in hell at any rate works *so as by fire*.

Over and above this material environment I have been myself led to argue the probability of the spiritual substance of the soul, or evil angel, itself coming truly to burn under two opposing constraints, the natural constraint, or effort, of the spirit, seeking to go out to God, easy to guess. The most intense pain known to man is caused by fire. We can no more form an adequate conception of the nature of eternal punishment and its medium than of the beatitude of Heaven,[33] and hence the sacred writer could hardly have chosen a more appropriate phrase than "Depart from me, ye cursed, into everlasting fire," [34] even in a context where metaphorical expressions are otherwise avoided. If Christ had called the infernal fire by its true name, we should not have understood His meaning as well as we do now.

in whom alone, as it finds out too late, its essential happiness lies, and to the contrary, the constraining hand of God, driving that spirit back upon itself. (By 'the constraining hand of God' I do not mean the 'material environment.' I mean simply God's will to carry out the sentence, 'Depart from me.'). Under analogous constraint, any material substance, as all physicists now know, would grow hot and glow intensely. The laws of matter may well have their analogue in the spirit world. If this be so, the mere *depart from me* must involve *everlasting fire.* If this be so again, the wicked spirit has made its own hell, having first rejected the God who now rejects it. Also, if this be so, it becomes transparently clear that as Heaven means *God,* so hell means *no God;* and no God is just what the obstinate impenitent sinner has chosen to have in this life, and consequently in the next. This, however, is a speculation. It makes the fire of hell very real and very terrible. For what is terrible in a fire is not the medium in which you are placed, but how you yourself burn.

"There are two perfectly distinct fires of hell, arising from quite distinct causes. There is first what I have called 'a material environment,' 'some external objective environment,' producing in the soul plunged into it a pain which to us, with our human experiences, is most properly declared by calling it the pain of fire. Of the nature of this material environment I have no idea, no theory, any more than St. Augustine had. I accept the fact of it simply because I wish to keep my rank in the common herd of Christian believers. Secondly, there is the loss of God; and about that, what I have had to say comes to this, that considering the relation in which the soul stands to its Last End, the mere felt loss of God, apart from all other agency, may, on an analogy drawn from the physical to the spiritual, be enough to set the substance of the soul veritably on fire. The 'mighty constraining force,' which I have invoked for this theory, is something quite over and above the 'material environment.' It is God's refusal of the soul, driving it away from Him, a refusal called a *force* only by analogy with things physical."

33 1 Cor. II, 9.

34 Matth. XXV, 41.

For all these reasons we deem it advisable to confess our ignorance in a matter that plainly exceeds human understanding, rather than engage in speculations which might easily lead us into error. Let us live so that we need not fear the mysterious fire of Hell.[35]

3. ACCIDENTAL PAINS OF THE DAMNED.—Besides the pain of loss and the pain of sense, which together constitute the essence of Hell, the damned suffer various accidental punishments. There is first and above all the remorse of conscience, which the Bible compares to a worm that will not die.[36] These are all the more terrible as the damned never experience the slightest alleviation of their suffering and are compelled to live forever with demons and witness their hideous outbursts of rage and hatred. The reunion of soul and body after the Resurrection will further increase the misery of the lost souls in Hell.

35 Cfr. Knabenbauer, *Comment. in Matth.*, Vol. II, pp. 384 sq., Paris 1894; Scheeben, *Die Mysterien des Christentums*, 3rd ed., pp. 607 sqq., Freiburg 1912.

36 Mark IX, 43.

SECTION 3

CHARACTERISTICS OF THE PAINS OF HELL

The pains of Hell have two distinguishing characteristics: (1) they are eternal and (2) they differ in degree according to guilt.

I. THE PAINS OF HELL ARE ETERNAL.—In consequence of the erroneous teaching of Origen, the Church early in her history defined the eternity of Hell as an article of faith. She did this at the Council of Constantinople, in 543. The definition given by this Council was approved by the Fifth Ecumenical Council of 553.[1] The Athanasian Creed, which was compiled about the same time, says: "They that have done good shall go into everlasting bliss, and they that have done evil, into everlasting fire." [2] This truth was repeated in similar terms by the Fourth Council of the Lateran.[3] The Protestant Reformers did not attack the dogma of eternal punishment, and hence the Tridentine Synod contented itself with declaring: "If any one saith that in every good

1 Cfr. Hefele, *Conciliengeschichte*, Vol. II, § 257.

2 " *Qui bona egerunt, ibunt in vitam aeternam, qui vero mala, in ig-*nem aeternum." (Denzinger-Bannwart, n. 40).

3 *V. supra*, p. 46.

work the just man sins, . . . and consequently deserves eternal punishments, . . . let him be anathema." [4]

a) The dogma of eternal punishment is clearly contained in Sacred Scripture. The prophet Daniel proclaims: "Many of those that sleep in the dust of the earth, shall awake: some unto life everlasting, and others unto reproach, to see it always." [5] The New Testament speaks repeatedly of an eternal and inextinguishable fire. [6] St. John says in the Apocalypse: "And the beast and the false prophet shall be tormented day and night for ever and ever." [7]

Though *saeculum* (αἰών) is sometimes used indefinitely to denote a period of long duration, [8] its meaning in this passage obviously is *eternity*. The phrase *in saecula saeculorum* always has this meaning in the New Testament, whether referring to the glory of God, [9] the kingdom of Christ, [10] or the joys of Heaven. [11] St. Augustine has pointed out that there is no stronger argument for the eternity of Hell than the fact that Sacred Scripture compares it in respect of duration to Heaven. [12] This rea-

---

[4] Sess. VI, can. 25: "*Si quis dixerit, iustum in quolibet opere bono peccare . . . atque ideo poenas aeternas mereri, anathema sit.*"

[5] Dan. XII, 2: "*Et multi de his, qui dormiunt in terrae pulvere, evigilabunt: alii in vitam aeternam, et alii in opprobrium ut videant semper.*"

[6] *V. supra*, Sect. 1.

[7] Apoc. XX, 10: "*. . . et bestia et pseudopropheta cruciabuntur die ac nocte in saecula saeculorum.*"

[8] Cfr. Pohle-Preuss, *God: His Knowability, Essence, and Attributes*, pp. 306 sqq.

[9] 1 Tim. I, 17; 2 Tim. IV, 18; Gal. I, 5; Apoc. XV, 7.

[10] Apoc. I, 18; XI, 15.

[11] Apoc. XXII, 5.

[12] *De Civitate Dei*, XXI, 23: "*Si utrumque aeternum, profecto aut utrumque cum fine diuturnum aut utrumque sine fine perpetuum debet intellegi; par pari enim relata sunt.*"

soning is confirmed by the Biblical teaching that the fate of every man is irrevocably sealed at death.[18] That there is no hope of salvation for the wicked in Hell may be concluded from our Saviour's dictum, " It were better for him if that man had never been born."[14]

b) The Fathers echo the teaching of Scripture. St. Polycarp tells his executioners: "You threaten me with fire, which burns but for an hour[15] and then is extinguished; for you know not the eternal fire of punishment reserved for the wicked."[16] Minucius Felix says: "There is neither measure nor termination to these torments. There the intelligent fire (πῦρ σωφρονοῦν) burns the limbs and restores them, feeds on them and nourishes them. . . . So that penal fire is not fed by the waste of those who burn, but is nourished by the unexhausted eating away of their bodies."[17]

Origen held that all free creatures, demons as well as lost souls, will ultimately share in the grace of salvation (apocatastasis). This heretical teaching to some extent influenced even such enlightened writers as Didymus the

13 V. supra, Sect. 1, No. 2, Thes. 3.

14 Matth. XXVI, 24: ". . . bonum erat ei, si natus non fuisset homo ille."

15 πρὸς ὥραν.

16 αἰώνιον κολάσεως πῦρ. (Martyr. Polyc., XI, 2; Funk, Patres Apost., I, 295).

17 Octavius, 35: " Nec tormentis aut modus ullus aut terminus. Illic sapiens ignis membra urit et reficit, carpit et nutrit. . . . Ita poenale illud incendium non damnis ardentium pascitur, sed inexesa corporum laceratione nutritur." Some editors have changed sapiens to rapiens, but there is no need of this, as πῦρ σωφρονοῦν is an expression of Clemens Alexandrinus. (See R. E. Wallis, The Writings of Cyprian, Vol. II, p. 509, n. 1, Edinburgh 1869). For additional Patristic testimonies see Petavius, De Angelis, III, 8, 4.

Blind, Evagrius of Pontus, and St. Gregory of Nyssa. It is not true, however,[18] as some writers assert, that St. Gregory of Nazianzus and St. Jerome denied the dogma of eternal punishment.[19]

c) The proposition, *"Ex inferno nulla redemptio,"* can be demonstrated also by theological reasoning. If it were possible to rescue a lost soul from Hell, this could only be in one of four ways: by conversion, by an apocatastasis in the sense of Origen, by complete annihilation, or through the intercession of the living.

The first and second of these methods have been excluded by positive arguments, which incidentally also prove the impossibility of the fourth. St. Augustine expressly says that the damned do not receive the slightest alleviation of their sufferings through the intercession of the living.[20] Some Fathers and theologians, particularly St. Chrysostom [21] and the poet Prudentius,[22] held that now and then, on stated days, as in the night before Easter, God grants the damned a certain respite through the prayers of the faithful. Petavius [23] judges this hypothesis mildly, whereas St. Thomas rejects it as vain, presumptuous, and without authority.[24] The singing of

18 Cfr. Kleinheidt, *Gregorii Nyss. Doctrina de Angelis,* pp. 48 sqq., Freiburg 1860; Hilt, *Des hl. Gregor von Nyssa Lehre vom Menschen,* Cologne 1890.

19 Cfr. Pesch, *Praelect. Dogmat.,* Vol. IX, 2nd ed., pp. 309 sqq.— On the eternity of Hell see Bautz, *Die Hölle,* 2nd ed., pp. 56 sqq., Mayence 1905.

20 *De Civitate Dei,* XXI, 24. Elsewhere, however (*e. g. Enchir.,* 110) he seems to take a different view.

21 *Hom. in Ep. ad Phil.,* 2, n. 3.

22 *Hymn.,* V, 125 sqq., in Migne, *P. L.,* LIX, 827.

23 *De Angelis,* III, 8.

24 *Summa Theol., Supplement.,* qu. 71, art. 5: " *Est praedicta opinio praesumptuosa, utpote dictis sancto·*

a certain hymn by St. Prudentius at the lighting of the Paschal candle is not equivalent to an ecclesiastical approval of the author's belief.[25] The only other means by which a reprobate could escape eternal punishment is complete annihilation. The Socinians thus interpret "the second death" of the Apocalypse. But this interpretation is contrary to the teaching of St. John. Cfr. Apoc. XIV, 11: "The smoke of their torments shall ascend up for ever and ever."[26] Apoc. XX, 14: "And hell and death were cast into the pool of fire; this is the second death."[27] St. Paul, too, plainly avers that the damned are punished forever. "The wicked," he says, "will pay the penalty of everlasting ruin, from before the face of the Lord and the glory of his might."[28] Tradition is equally positive. St. Cyprian declares that the fire of Hell is everlasting and no respite is granted to the damned.[29] St. Gregory, in a characteristic passage of his *Expositio in Librum Job,* generally known by the title of *Moralia,* calls Hell " *mors sine morte, finis sine fine, defectus sine defectu, quia et mors vivit et finis semper incipit et deficere defectus nescit."* [30]

d) Philosophy cannot furnish conclusive evidence for the eternity of Hell, but it can show that this truth is not repugnant to reason and

---

rum contraria et vana, nullâ auctoritate fulta."
25 Cfr. H. Hurter, S.J., *Compendium Theologiae Dogmat.,* Vol. III, n. 808.
26 Apoc. XIV, 11: καὶ ὁ καπνὸς τοῦ βασανισμοῦ αὐτῶν εἰς αἰῶνας αἰώνων ἀναβαίνει.
27 Apoc. XX, 14: καὶ ὁ θάνατος καὶ ἄδης ἐβλήθησαν εἰς τὴν λίμνην τοῦ πυρός· οὗτος ὁ θάνατος ὁ δεύτερός ἐστιν(Cfr. Apoc. XXI, 8.)

28 2 Thess. I, 9: " *Qui poenas dabunt in interitu aeternas* (δίκην τίσουσιν ὅλεθρον αἰώνιον) *a facie Domini et a gloria virtutis eius."*
29 *Ad Demetr.,* 24: " *Cremabit addictos ardens semper gehenna ct vivacibus flammis vorax poena. Nec erit, unde habere tormenta vel requiem possint aliquando vel finem."*
30 *Moralia,* IX, 66.

that the objections raised against it prove nothing.

a) When the wicked soul enters into the *status termini*, it realizes that it is irrevocably lost. God, who alone could save it, refuses to do so. "He who falls into mortal sin by his own free will," says St. Thomas, "puts himself into a state from which he cannot be rescued except with the help of God, just as one who casts himself into an abyss from which he could not escape unaided, might say that it was his will to stay there forever, no matter what else he may have thought."[31] The final decision being irrevocable, the will is confirmed in malice and can no longer feel contrition.[32]

Moreover, punishment must be coextensive with guilt. The guilt of mortal sin consists in the deprivation of grace, which loss, for those who have entered upon the *status termini*, is irretrievable, and consequently the *reatus poenae*, too, must be eternal. "Therefore," says St. Thomas, "whatever sins turn man away from God, so as to destroy charity, considered in themselves, incur a debt of eternal punishment."[33]

β) It has been objected that there is no proportion between a sinful act or thought, which lasts but one brief moment, and eternal punishment. The comparison is not correctly drawn. Though the sinful act (*peccatum*

---

31 *Summa Theol., Supplement.*, qu. 99, art. 1: "*Qui in peccatum mortale labitur propriâ voluntate, se ponit in statu, a quo erui non potest nisi divinitus adiutus; sicut si aliquis se in foveam proiiceret, unde exire non posset, nisi adiutus, posset dici quod in aeternum ibi manere voluerit, quantumcunque aliter cogitaret.*"

32 Cfr. *Op. cit.*, qu. 98, art. 1 sqq.

33 *Summa Theol.*, 1a 2ae, qu. 87, art. 3: "*Et ideo quaecunque peccata avertunt a Deo caritatem auferentia, quantum est de se, inducunt reatum aeternae poenae.*"— Other arguments *apud* Sachs, *Die ewige Dauer der Höllenstrafen,* Paderborn 1900.

actuale) be brief and transient, the ensuing sinful *habitus* or state endures. St. Thomas explains this with his wonted lucidity as follows: " The fact that adultery or murder is committed in a moment, does not call for a momentary punishment; in fact, these crimes are sometimes punished by imprisonment or banishment for life, sometimes even by death; . . . this punishment, in its own way, represents the eternity of punishment inflicted by God." [34]

The so-called *misericordes,* whom St. Augustine combatted,[35] appealed to the mercy of God as an argument against eternal punishment. But God is not only merciful, He is also infinitely just and holy, and His justice and holiness compel Him to hate and punish sin in proportion to its guilt. The divine mercy is not a weakly sentimentality, but benevolent goodness tempered by strict justice. If there were any chance of conversion in the other world, or any hope that Hell might end, even after millions of years, how few would shrink from sin! [36] The thought of eternal punishment alone deters the average man from crime.

St. Gregory of Nyssa's friendly attitude towards Origen's theory of a universal apocatastasis is explicable on the assumption that he regarded the reform of the evildoer as the sole object of punishment. This view is incorrect. Punishment is inflicted primarily to satisfy divine justice and to vindicate and restore the disturbed moral order (*poena vindicativa*).[37] Not even worldly

34 *Summa Theol.,* 1a 2ae, qu. 87, art. 3, ad 1: "*Non enim quia adulterium vel homicidium in momento committitur, propter hoc momentaneâ poenâ punitur, sed quandoque quidem perpetuo carcere vel exilio, quandoque etiam morte,* . . . *et sic repraesentat suo modo aeterni-*

tatem poenae divinitus inflictae."
35 *De Civitate Dei,* XXI, 18, 1.
36 Cfr. St. Jerome, *In Ioa.,* 3, 6 (Migne, *P. L.,* XXV, 1142).
37 Cfr. Pohle-Preuss, *God: His Knowability, Essence, and Attributes,* pp. 460 sqq.

justice can get along without vindictive punishments, though Lombroso and Liszt have tried to abolish them by declaring all crimes to be the result of bodily disease or mental disorder. "Even the punishment that is inflicted according to human laws," says St. Thomas, "is not always intended as a medicine for the one who is punished, but sometimes only for others. Thus when a thief is hanged, this is not done for his own amendment, but for the sake of others, that at least they may be deterred from crime through fear of punishment." [38]

Another objection raised against the dogma of eternal punishment is based upon the desire for happiness which the Creator has implanted in every human heart. But God is not obliged to gratify this desire in all men. He has conditioned eternal happiness upon a good life. If the innate desire for happiness remains unsatisfied in some, it is their fault, not God's.

It is true that the happiness of rational creatures is the secondary purpose of creation; but, as we have seen in a previous treatise,[39] this purpose is subordinate to the glory of God (*gloria Dei*), which is attained by the manifestation of His justice no less than His mercy.

2. THE PAINS OF HELL DIFFER IN DEGREE ACCORDING TO GUILT.—Though one single mortal sin renders the sinner as deserving of Hell as a thousand crimes, justice demands that sins be punished in proportion to their grievousness. Ac-

---

[38] *Summa Theol.*, 1a 2ae, qu. 87, art. 3, ad 2: "*Poena, quae etiam secundum leges humanas infligitur, non semper est medicinalis ei, qui punitur, sed solum aliis; sicut quum latro suspenditur, non ut ipse emen-detur, sed propter alios, ut saltem metu poenae peccare desistant.*"

[39] Pohle-Preuss, *God the Author of Nature and the Supernatural*, pp. 80 sqq.

cordingly, to the degrees of reward and happiness enjoyed by the Blessed in Heaven there correspond analogous degrees of punishment and misery in Hell. This is the express teaching of the Church.[40]

a) Our Divine Saviour draws a clear-cut distinction between the judgment pronounced on Tyre and Sidon and the penalty inflicted on the unbelieving inhabitants of Corozain and Bethsaida. The inspired seer of the Apocalypse says of the corrupt city of Babylon: "Render to her even as herself hath rendered, and give her double according to her works; . . . as much as she hath glorified herself and wantoned in luxury, so much give her of torment and mourning." [41] Cfr. Wisd. VI, 7 sqq.: ". . . the mighty shall be mightily tormented, . . . a greater punishment is ready for the more mighty." [42]

b) The Fathers seem to have held that the *poena damni,* being a mere privation, is inflicted equally on all, but that the *poenae sensus* differ in degree. Thus St. Gregory the Great says: "As there are many mansions in the house of the Father, according to the different degrees of virtue, so the disparity of guilt subjects the damned

40 "*Poenis tamen disparibus.*" (*Conc. Florent.*, A. D. 1439).

41 Apoc. XVIII, 6 sq.: "*Reddite illi sicut et ipsa reddidit vobis: et duplicate ei duplicia secundum opera eius; . . . quantum glorificavit se et in deliciis fuit, tantum date illi tormentum et luctum.*"

42 "*Potentes autem potenter tormenta patientur, . . . fortioribus, autem fortior instat cruciatio.*"

in different degrees to the fire of Hell." [43]   Dante
exemplifies this belief in the concentric circles of
his Inferno.   Of course only a mysterious and
essentially supernatural fire can produce such
radically different effects.

READINGS: — Patuzzi, *De Futuro Impiorum Statu*, Venice 1749.
—Carle, *Du Dogme Catholique sur l'Enfer*, Paris 1842.—J.
Bautz, *Die Hölle*, 2nd ed., Mayence 1905.—L. de Ségur, *L'Enfer*,
39th ed., Paris 1905 (German tr., *Die Hölle*, 3rd ed., Mayence
1889.) —Fr. Schmid, *Quaestiones Selectae ex Theologia Dog-
matica*, pp. 145 sqq., Paderborn 1891.—Tournelize, *Opinions du
Jour sur les Peines d'Outre-tombe: Feu Métaphorique, Univer-
salisme, Conditionalisme, Mitigation*, Paris 1899.— Passaglia, *De
Aeternitate Poenarum deque Igne Inferno*, Rome 1854.— J. Sachs,
Die ewige Dauer der Höllenstrafen, Paderborn 1900.— C. Gutber-
let, "*Die Poena Sensus*," in the Mayence *Katholik*, 1901, II, 305
sqq.— F. X. Kiefl, *Die Ewigkeit der Hölle und ihre spekulative
Begründung*, Paderborn 1905.— J. Hontheim, S.J., art. "Hell," in
the *Catholic Encyclopedia*, Vol. VII, pp. 207–211.— Card. Billot,
De Novissimis, Rome 1902.— Hewitt, "*Ignus Aeternus*," in the
Catholic World, LXVII (1893), pp. 426 sqq.— V. Morton,
Thoughts on Hell; A Study in Eschatology, London 1899.— Jos.
Rickaby, S.J., *Everlasting Punishment*, London 1916.— *Dublin
Review*, Jan. 1881.— Charles R. Roche, S.J., "Eternal Punish-
ment," in the *Irish Theological Quarterly*, Vol. V (1910), No. 17,
pp. 64–79.

[43] *Moral.*, IV, 47: "*Sicut in
domo Patris mansiones multae sunt
pro diversitate virtutis, sic damnatos*   *diverso supplicio gehennae ignibus
subiicit disparitas criminis.*"

CHAPTER V

PURGATORY

SECTION 1

THE EXISTENCE OF PURGATORY

1. DEFINITION.—Purgatory (*purgatorium*) signifies a process of cleansing.

a) Whether it is a place or a state is a controverted question. The poor souls are in a state of transition, but it is not necessary to hold that they are confined in any particular place. St. Thomas intimates that Purgatory is somehow " connected with Hell." [1] We might with equal probability argue that it is connected with Heaven, because the poor souls are children of God, who are sure sooner or later to be admitted to the abode of the Blessed. [2]

b) Not all who depart this life in the state of grace are fit to enter forthwith into the beatific vision of God. Some are burdened with venial transgressions. Others have not yet fully ex-

[1] *Summa Theol., Appendix*, qu. 1, art. 2.

[2] The various views regarding the location of Purgatory are set forth by Cardinal Bellarmine in his treat- ise, *De Purgatorio*, II, 6. That Purgatory is situated in the bowels of the earth is as undemonstrable as the location of Heaven and Hell.

piated the temporal punishments due to their sins.[3]
It would be repugnant to divine justice to admit
such souls to Heaven, into which, according to
Holy Writ, nothing defiled shall enter.[4] Nor can
God in his justice consign these souls to Hell.
Hence there must be a middle state in which they
are cleansed of venial sins, or, if they have not yet
fully paid the temporal punishments due to their
forgiven sins, must expiate the remainder of
them. St. Thomas says: "There may be some
impediment on the part of the good in the way of
their souls receiving their final reward in the vision of God immediately upon their departure from
the body. To that vision, transcending as it does
all natural created capacity, the creature cannot
be raised before it is entirely purified: hence it is
said that nothing defiled can enter into it (Wisd.
VII, 25), and that the polluted shall not pass
through it (Is. XXXV, 8). Now the pollution
of the soul is by sin, which is an inordinate union
with lower things; from which pollution it is purified in this life by Penance and other Sacraments.
Now it happens sometimes that this process of
purification is not entirely accomplished in this
life, and the offender remains still a debtor with a
debt of punishment upon him, owing to some neg-

3 Cfr. *Concil. Trident.*, Sess. IV,
can. 30; Pohle-Preuss, *The Sacraments*, Vol. III, p. 219.
4 Apoc. XXI, 27: "*Non intrabit*

in eam [*scil. civitatem*] *aliquod coin-
quinatum, aut abominationem fa-
ciens, et mendacium . . .*"

ligence or distraction, or to death overtaking him before his debt is paid. Not for this does he deserve to be entirely shut out from reward: because all this may happen without mortal sin, and it is only mortal sin that occasions the loss of charity, to which the reward of life everlasting is due. Such persons, then, must be cleansed in the next life, before entering upon their eternal reward. This cleansing is done by penal inflictions, as even in this life it might have been completed by penal works of satisfaction: otherwise the negligent would be better off than the careful, if the penalty that men do not pay here for their sins is not to be undergone by them in the life to come. The souls, then, of the good, who have upon them in this world something that needs cleansing, are kept back from their reward, while they endure cleansing purgatorial pains. And this is the reason why we posit a purgatory or place of cleansing." [5]

Purgatory may therefore be defined as a state of temporary punishment for those who, departing this life in the grace of God, are not entirely free from venial sins or have not yet fully paid the satisfaction due to their transgressions.

2. PROOF FROM REVELATION.—The existence of Purgatory was denied by Aërius in the fourth

century, by the Albigenses, Waldenses, and Hussites in the Middle Ages, and more recently by Luther and Calvin.[6]   Calvin termed the Catholic dogma " a pernicious invention of Satan, which renders the cross of Christ useless." [7]   This teaching of the Reformers is quite consistent with their false idea of justification. If a man is justified by faith alone, and all his sins are "covered up" by the grace of Christ, there can be nothing left for him to expiate after death.

The Church defined the existence of Purgatory in the Decree of Union adopted at Florence (1439), by saying that "the souls are cleansed by purgatorial pains after death, and in order that they may be rescued from these pains, they are benefitted by the suffrages of the living faithful, *viz.:* the sacrifice of the Mass, prayers, alms, and other works of piety." [8]   The Council of Trent repeated this definition in substance: ". . . The Catholic Church, instructed by the Holy Ghost, has, from the sacred writings and the ancient tradition of the Fathers, taught in sacred councils, and very recently in this ecumenical Synod,[9] that there is a Purgatory, and that the souls detained

6 Cfr. Bellarmine, *De Purgatorio,* I, 2.

7 " *Exitiale satanae commentum, quod Christi crucem evacuat.*" (*Inst.,* III, 5, § 6).

8 " *Animas poenis purgatoriis post mortem purgari et, ut a poenis hu-* iusmodi releventur, prodesse eis fidelium vivorum suffragia, missarum scil. sacrificia, orationes et elemosynas et alia pietatis officia." (Denzinger-Bannwart, n. 693).

9 Sess. VI, can. 30; Sess. XXII, cap. 2 and 3.

in it are helped by the suffrages of the faithful." [10] Pope Leo X solemnly condemned Luther's assertion that "Purgatory cannot be proved
from the canonical Scriptures." [11]

a) The scriptural *locus classicus* for our
dogma is 2 Mach. XII, 43 sqq. When Judas had
put Gorgias to flight, and came with his company
to take away the bodies of the slain, he found that
some of them had under their coats treasures
which they had robbed from the idols of Jamnia.
In committing this robbery the soldiers had
probably been moved by avarice rather than
idolatrous intent. Yet their conduct was plainly
a transgression of the Mosaic law, which said:
"Their graven things thou shalt burn with fire;
thou shalt not covet the silver and gold of which
they are made, neither shalt thou make to thee any
thing thereof, lest thou offend, because it is an
abomination to the Lord thy God." [12] However,
what these soldiers had done was not necessarily a
mortal sin, and so Judas and his men, after blessing the just judgment of God, betook themselves
to prayer, and "making a gathering [taking up
a collection], he sent twelve thousand drachmas
of silver to Jerusalem for sacrifice to be offered
for the sins of the dead." Both Judas and his

---

10 Sess. XXV: "*Purgatorium
esse animasque ibi detentas fidelium
suffragiis, potissimum vero acceptabili altaris sacrificio iuvari.*" (Denzinger-Bannwart, n. 983).

11 Prop. Damn. a Leone X., prop.
37: "*Purgatorium non potest pro-
bari ex Scriptura, quae sit in ca-
none.*"

12 Deut. VII, 25.

people, as well as the priests of the Temple, evidently believed that those who die in the grace of God can obtain forgiveness of venial sins and temporal punishments through the suffrages of the living. This belief is confirmed by the sacred writer when he adds: "It is therefore a holy and wholesome thought [13] to pray for the dead, that they may be loosed from sins." [14]

Protestants deny the cogency of this argument on the ground that the Book of Machabees is apocryphal. But the historical authenticity of the incident sufficiently proves that belief in Purgatory, so far from being an invention of the " Papists," was common among the Jews long before the beginning of the Christian era. [15]

From the New Testament we will quote the remarkable utterance of our Lord recorded in Matth. XII, 32: "Whosoever shall speak . . . against the Holy Ghost, it shall not be forgiven him neither in this world, nor in the world to come." [16] The "world to come" (αἰὼν μέλλων) plainly means life after death. Hence, according to our Saviour's own testimony, there must be some sins that are forgiven after death. [17]

---

13 ὁσία καὶ εὐσεβὴς ἐπίνοια.
14 τῆς ἁμαρτίας ἀπολυθῆναι. (2 Mach. XII, 45).
15 Cfr. Mayer, *Das Judentum*, pp. 465 sqq., Ratisbon 1893.
16 Matth. XII, 32: " *Qui autem dixerit* [*verbum*] *contra Spiritum sanctum, non remittetur ei neque in hoc saeculo neque in futuro.*"

17 This interpretation is favored by Augustine .(*De Civ. Dei*, XXI, 24) and other Fathers (see Hurter, *Compendium Theol. Dogmat.*, Vol. III, n. 823). St. Gregory the Great, e. g., teaches: " *In qua sententia datur intelligi, quasdam culpas in hoc saeculo, quasdam vero in futuro posse relaxari.*" (*Dial.*, IV, 29).

b) The belief of the early Church is evident from the immemorial custom of praying for the dead, offering the Holy Sacrifice, and giving alms for their benefit.

Tertullian mentions anniversary masses for the dead.[18] That he had Purgatory in mind appears from his advice to a widow, " to pray for the soul of her husband, begging repose for him, and . . . to have sacrifice offered up for him every year on the day of his death." [19] This pious custom is confirmed by many sepulchral inscriptions found in the catacombs, in which the departed ask for the prayers of their surviving friends or beg God for " peace and refreshment." [20] The Fathers expressly inculcate the doctrine which inspired these pious practices. In the Acts of St. Perpetua we read that she beheld her brother Dinocrates, who had died a heathen and was " suffering terrible torments, released from the place of punishment through her prayers." [21] St. Basil affirms the existence of " a place for the purification of souls " and of " a cleansing fire." [22] St. Augustine appeals to his friends to pray for his pious mother, St. Monica, and instructs them as to the most effective way of helping her soul.[23] There is no doubt," he says in another place, " that the dead are

18 *De Corona Mil.*, 3: " Oblationes pro defunctis annuâ die facimus."

19 *De Monogamia*, 10: " Debet pro anima eius orare et refrigerium interim adpostulare ei et . . . offerre annuis diebus dormitionis suae."— For other Patristic testimonies see Pohle-Preuss, *The Sacraments*, Vol. II, pp. 376 sq.

20 " Pax et refrigeratio," as e. g. in the formula: " Spiritum tuum Deus refrigeret."— Cfr. Kraus, *Realenzyklopädie der christlichen Altertümer*, Vol. II, s. v. " Refrigerium," Freiburg 1886; J. P. Kirsch, *Die Akklamationen und Gebete der altchristlichen Grabinschriften*, Cologne 1898.

21 *Acta Martyr. S. Perpetuae et Socior.*

22 χωρίον καθαρισμοῦ ψυχῶν; — καθάρσιον πῦρ. (*In Is.*, IX, 19).

23 *Confess.*, IX, 13.

aided by the prayers of holy Church, by the salutary sacrifice, and by the alms which are poured out for their souls." [24]

These passages from the writings of the Fathers could easily be multiplied. Even Calvin was constrained to admit that the custom of praying for the dead may be traced to the early days of Christianity.[25] Thinking Protestants keenly feel the gap in their theological system caused by the denial of Purgatory. Thus Dr. Hase says: " Most people when they die are probably too good for Hell, yet surely too bad for Heaven. It must be frankly confessed that the Protestantism of the Reformers is unclear on this point, its justified denial [?] not yet having advanced to the stage of affirmation." [26] The Catholic dogma in this as in so many other cases agrees perfectly with the postulates of reason.

24 *Sermones*, 172: " *Orationibus sanctae Ecclesiae et sacrificio salutari et ·elemosynis, quae pro eorum spiritibus erogantur, non est dubitandum mortuos adiuvari, ut cum eis misericordius agatur a Domino, quam eorum peccata meruerunt; hoc enim a Patribus traditum universa observat Ecclesia."* (Cfr. the same writer's *Enchirid.*, 60).— The argument from Tradition is developed more fully by Pesch, *Praelect. Dogmat.*, Vol. IX, 2nd ed., pp. 283 sqq.

25 *Inst.*, III, 5, § 10: " *Ante mille et trecentos annos usu receptum fuit, ut precationes fierent pro defunctis."*

26 *Handbuch der protestantischen Polemik gegen die römisch-kath. Kirche*, p. 445, Leipzig 1862: " *Die meisten Sterbenden sind wohl zu gut für die Hölle, aber sicher zu schlecht für den Himmel. Man muss offen zugestehen, dass hier im reformatorischen Protestantismus eine Unklarheit vorliegt, indem seine berechtigte Verneinung noch nicht zur Bejahung fortgeschritten war."*

SECTION 2

NATURE AND DURATION OF PURGATORY

The Church has defined nothing with regard to the nature of Purgatory except that the poor souls detained there are in a passing state of punishment and suffer "purgatorial pains."[1] Like the pains of Hell, those of Purgatory are twofold, *viz.:* pain of loss (*poena damni*) and pain of sense (*poena sensus*).

1. THE PAIN OF LOSS.—The *poena damni* for the poor souls in Purgatory consists in their being deprived of the beatific vision of God. This temporary deprivation constitutes the essence of the state of purgation. It is the severest punishment that can be inflicted upon a disembodied soul. The consciousness of being separated from the Creator, who is so near and yet so far, causes terrible suffering, which is enhanced still more by the knowledge that the venial sins and punishments due to sin could have been expiated by contrition, confession, prayer, almsgiving, and other good works so easily performed in the wayfaring state.

[1] "*Poenis purgatoriis;*" *v. supra*, p. 78.

Nevertheless, their sad condition does not drive the suffering souls to despair or to commit new sins, as Luther falsely claimed.[2]

For the rest, it would be no easier to write a psychology of the poor souls in Purgatory than of the damned in Hell. We earthly pilgrims are incapable of forming an adequate conception of the spiritual suffering involved in even a temporary privation of the beatific vision. Shorn of all earthly impediments, and placed beyond the world of sense which veils the things of the spirit, the poor souls in Purgatory concentrate their attention on God. But God hides and withdraws from them, which causes them to be tormented incessantly by a veritable agony of love. There is nothing improbable in St. Bonaventure's conjecture that " the severest pain of Purgatory exceeds the most violent known on earth," [3] but we need not necessarily adopt the opinion of St. Thomas that " even the slightest torture of Purgatory is worse than all the sufferings one can endure in this world." [4] There is no certainty to be had in these matters.[5]

2. THE PAIN OF SENSE.—Whether besides the *poena damni* the poor souls suffer a *poena sensus*, is doubtful. Still more difficult is it to answer the question whether this additional punishment, if it exist, is caused by a material medium similar to the fire of Hell. Theologians

---

[2] *Prop. Damn. a Leone X,* prop. 38: *"Animae in purgatorio non sunt securae de earum salute, saltem non omnes."*—Prop. 39: *"Animae in purgatorio peccant sine intermissione, quamdiu quaerunt requiem et horrent poenas."*

[3] *Comment. in Sent.,* IV, dist. 20, art. 1, qu. 2.

[4] *Comment. in Sent.,* IV, dist. 21, qu. 1, art. 1.

[5] Cfr. Bellarmine, *De Purgatorio,* II, 14.

consider it extremely probable that such is the case.

a) The phrase employed by the Florentine Council, *"animas poenis purgatoriis purgari,"* seems to point to the existence of some positive torment over and above the *poena damni.* This assumption gains strength from the concurrent teaching of the Fathers and Schoolmen.

The difficulty begins when we attempt to ascertain the precise nature of the sensitive pain experienced by the poor souls. The Church has issued no definition with regard to the existence of a purgatorial fire, and hence nothing can be asserted on this head as of faith or even as *fidei proximum.* When Cardinal Bessarion at the Council of Florence argued against the existence of a real fire in Purgatory, the Greeks were assured that the Roman Church had never pronounced dogmatically on the subject, and nothing was said about it in the Decree of Union. The Greek view that Purgatory is a place of darkness, smoke, and mourning (*locus caliginis, tenebrarum, turbinis, moeroris*) is too vague to enable us to form any positive idea as to its nature.[6]

b) In the Western Church belief in the existence of a material purgatorial fire, analogous to the fire of a Hell, is common. Hence the name *"ignis purgatorius"* (German, *Fegefeuer*). This view derives a certain probability from 1 Cor. III, 11 sqq.

6 On the teaching of the Russian schismatics see A. Bukowski, S.J., *Die Genugtuung für die Sünde nach der Auffassung der russischen Orthodoxie,* pp. 143 sqq., Paderborn 1911.

a) In warning the faithful of Corinth against certain dangerous doctrines that were propagated among them, the Apostle says: " Foundation can no man lay other than that which is [already] laid, which is Jesus Christ. But if a man buildeth upon the foundation, [whether it be] gold, silver, precious stones, wood, grass [or] straw,— the work of each man shall become manifest. For the Day shall declare it, because [that day] is to be disclosed in fire, and the worth of each man's work shall that fire assay. If any man's work abide, which he hath built thereupon, he shall receive reward: if any man's work be burnt up, he shall lose his reward, but himself shall be saved, yet as [one that hath passed] through fire." [7]   No doubt the test by fire is quite as much a figure of speech as building upon a foundation of gold, silver, precious stones, wood, grass or straw. But the concluding sentence, which asserts that a man shall be saved *as through fire*, seems to indicate that there is a real fire in Purgatory.[8]

β) The Pauline passage is interpreted literally by some of the Fathers. Thus St. Ambrose writes: " When Paul says, ' yet as through fire,' he means that he will indeed be saved, but will have to suffer the pain of fire, in order that, purged by fire, he be saved." [9]   St. Augustine, on

[7] 1 Cor. III, 12 sqq.: Εἰ δέ τις ἐποικοδομεῖ ἐπὶ τὸν θεμέλιον τοῦτον χρυσόν, ἄργυρον, λίθους τιμίους, ξύλα, χόρτον, καλάμην, ἑκάστου τὸ ἔργον φανερὸν γενήσεται· ἡ γὰρ ἡμέρα δηλώσει, ὅτι ἐν πυρὶ ἀποκαλύπτεται, καὶ ἑκάστου τὸ ἔργον ὁποῖόν ἐστιν, τὸ πῦρ δοκιμάσει. Εἴ τινος τὸ ἔργον μενεῖ ὃ ἐποικοδόμησεν, μισθὸν λήμψεται· εἴ τινος τὸ ἔργον κατακαήσεται, ζημιωθήσεται, αὐτὸς δὲ σωθήσεται, οὕτως δὲ ὡς διὰ πυρός.
[8] On 1 Cor. III, 11 sqq., see Bell-

armine, *De Purgatorio*, I, 5; Al. Schäfer, *Erklärung der beiden Briefe an die Korinther*, pp. 70 sqq.; J. MacRory, *The Epistles of St. Paul to the Corinthians*, Part I, pp. 38 sqq.; Hugh Pope, O.P., in the *Irish Theol. Quarterly*, Vol. IV (1909), No. 16, pp. 441–456.
[9] *In Ps.*, 118: "*Quum Paulus dicit:* ' *sic tamen, quasi per ignem, ostendit quidem illum salvum futurum, sed poenam ignis passurum, ut per ignem purgatus fiat salvus.*"

the other hand, interprets the phrase " *quasi per ignem* " figuratively, applying it to " the fiery furnace of earthly tribulations." Origen says: " Whoever is saved, is saved through fire, in order that, if he contains an admixture of dross, it be dissolved by fire, so that all may become solid gold." [10] This passage and another similar one in Origen's writings [11] show that he regarded the purgatorial fire as a figure of speech. In this he followed his master, Clement of Alexandria, who called Purgatory " a spiritual fire." [12] On the whole it may be said that the number of Greek Fathers who believe in the existence of a real fire in Purgatory is quite small. Among the Fathers of the Latin Church some favor the literal interpretation. Thus St. Gregory the Great speaks of those who after this life " will expiate their faults by purgatorial flames," and adds that the pain will be more intense than any that can be suffered in this life.[13] In another place he says: " But it must be believed that there is a purgatorial fire for [the expiation of] venial sins before the [General] Judgment." [14] But even in the West there is not a sufficient *consensus patrum* for a solid argument from Tradition.

γ) This fact did not, however, prevent the Scholastics from confidently asserting the existence of a material fire in Purgatory. The value of their teaching is discounted by the fact that they were uncritical, ascribed too much importance to unauthenticated visions and private revelations, and tried to prove the reality of the purgatorial fire from the existence of volcanoes, and so forth. We need not wonder, in view of such insufficient argu-

---

10 *Hom. in Exod.*, 6.
11 *De Principiis*, II, 10.
12 τὸ φρόνιμον πῦρ. (*Stromata*, VII, 6).
13 *Ps. III Poenit.*, n. 1.

14 *Dial.*, IV, 39: " *Sed tamen de quibusdam levibus culpis ante iudicium* [*universale*] *esse purgatorius ignis credendus est.*"

ments, that a number of modern theologians (*e. g.* Klee, Möhler, Dieringer) deny, or at least doubt, the existence of a material fire in Purgatory. However, it is well to remember, in the words of Cardinal Bellarmine, that " If there is no real fire, there will be something much more terrible, which God has prepared in order to demonstrate His power." [15]

3. How the Poor Souls are Cleansed in Purgatory.—Clement of Alexandria taught [16] that the poor souls can effect their own spiritual amendment by submitting patiently to the torments of Purgatory. [17] Whatever we may hold on this subject, one thing is certain, namely, that no merits can be acquired in Purgatory. [18]

A more important and more practical problem is, how the poor souls expiate their venial sins and the punishments due to their forgiven mortal sins, and how they get rid of their evil habits.

a) Forgiveness of venial sins can be obtained in three different ways: (1) by unconditional remission on the part of God; (2) by suffering and the performance of penitential works, and (3) by an act of contrition.

(1) Absolutely speaking, God can forgive all sins unconditionally. But in the present economy He has chosen to make contrition a condition of forgiveness, and hence it

---

15 *De Purg.*, II, 14: " *Si ibi est verus ignis, erit omnino acerrimus . . . si non ignis verus, erit aliquid multo horribilius, quale Deus parare potuit, qui potentiam suam in hoc* ostendere *voluit.*"
16 See *Stromata*, VII, 12.
17 δευτέρα παιδεία.
18 Cfr. Oswald, *Eschatologie*, p. 119.

is not reasonable to suppose that venial sins are forgiven unconditionally in Purgatory.

(2) What does God demand of the poor souls as a condition of forgiveness? Can it be mere passive suffering (*satispassio*)? This might wipe out the *reatus poenae*, but it could never wipe out the *reatus culpae*, of which a sinner can rid himself only by an act of contrition (*motus displicentiae*). Hence the only means by which venial sins can be forgiven in Purgatory is contrition. St. Thomas says: " Venial sins are remitted after this life, even with regard to guilt, in the same way in which they are remitted in this life, namely, by an act of charity towards God, expressing repugnance for the venial sins committed in this life. However, since it is no longer possible to acquire merits in the world beyond, such an act of love, while it removes the impediment of venial guilt, does not deserve absolution or a decrease of punishment." [19]

When does the soul make the act of contrition which wipes out venial sin? Most probably immediately after its separation from the body, when the soul is for the first time alone with God.[20] Some theologians, however, think that the process of purgation is gradual.[21]

b) It is not difficult to understand how the temporal punishments due to sin are expiated in Purgatory. The soul is no longer able to make satis-

---

[19] *De Malo*, qu. 7, art. 11: " *Venialia remittuntur eis post hanc vitam etiam quantum ad culpam eo modo, quo remittuntur in hac vita, scil. per actum caritatis in Deum repugnantem venialibus in hac vita commissis. Quia tamen post hanc vitam non est status merendi, ille* dilectionis motus in eis tollit quidem impedimentum venialis culpae, non tamen meretur absolutionem vel diminutionem poenae.*"

[20] Cfr. Suarez, *Comment in S. Theol.*, III, disp. 11, sect. 4.

[21] Cfr. Fr. Schmid, *Die Seelenläuterung im Jenseits*, Brixen 1907.

faction, and hence can atone only by suffering.
This suffering, technically called *satispassio*,[22]
has neither meritorious nor satisfactory value because the poor souls are no longer able to do anything for themselves, but have entered into the
night "in which no man can labor."

The *duration* of Purgatory is entirely a matter of conjecture. Some theologians think that the poor souls are
detained for a long time; others, that the period of
purgation is brief. The truth probably lies between
these two extremes. God, being infinitely just, owes it
to Himself to punish every sin according to its guilt and
to exclude from Heaven whatever is unclean. But He
is also infinitely merciful, and His mercy has provided
an effective means of shortening the sufferings of the
poor souls through the intercession of the Church and
the faithful on earth.

Dominicus Soto and Maldonatus maintained that no
one remains in Purgatory longer than ten years. This
view is untenable, and one of the practical conclusions
drawn from it, namely, that legacies for the saying of
masses for the dead become invalid after ten years, has
been formally condemned by Alexander VII.[23] However, from her acceptance of unlimited mass stipends it
does not follow that the Church believes the sufferings of
the poor souls in Purgatory to be of extremely long duration. God, in consideration of a great number of masses
and suffrages which He has foreseen from all eternity,
may release a soul immediately after death. On the other

22 On the nature of *satispassio* see
St. Bonaventure, *Comment. in Sent.*,
IV, dist. 20, p. 1, art. 1, qu. 3.
23 *Prop. Damn. die 18. Martii,*
1666, prop. 43: "*Annuum legatum
pro anima relictum non durat plus
quam per decem annos.*" (Denzinger-Bannwart, n. 1143).

hand, no one can be sure that Purgatory does not last for centuries in the case of souls who enter eternity with an exceptionally heavy load of venial sins and temporal punishments. The faithful who will be alive at the second coming of our Lord will not, of course, be able to expiate their venial sins and temporal punishments in Purgatory, for there will be no Purgatory after the Last Judgment. With regard to these survivors it is piously believed that God will grant them a general indulgence, or that the tribulations and sufferings they will have to undergo will make up for their deficiencies.

c) A word concerning the evil habits which remain in the soul after conversion.

There are two classes of evil habits (*habitus*), *viz.*: those which are rooted in the sensitive faculties (drunkenness, impurity, etc.), and those which are based on the spiritual powers of the will (pride, excessive ambition, etc.). The former are eradicated as it were automatically at the moment of death, when the sensitive faculties become inoperative. The latter accompany the soul into Purgatory, but are probably destroyed by an act of love elicited at the threshold of eternity. Should these habits continue to exist in Purgatory, there can be no doubt that they are eventually cast off at the gate of Heaven. They cannot be expiated by suffering because they have already been the subject of contrition, and, like concupiscence, are neither sins nor deserving of punishment.

SECTION 3

SUCCORING THE DEAD

1. THE DOGMA OF THE COMMUNION OF SAINTS.—The Council of Trent says that the poor souls in Purgatory "are aided by the suffrages of the faithful, and principally by the acceptable sacrifice of the altar."[1] The efficacy of this intercession is based on the Communion of Saints.[2]

a) By the Communion of Saints we understand the spiritual union of the faithful with one another, with the blessed Angels, the Elect in Heaven, and the poor souls in Purgatory, under the supernatural headship of Christ, who is the font and well-spring of all grace;[3] or, to put it somewhat differently, the mystic union of the militant, the triumphant, and the suffering Church of Christ.

b) The ninth article of the Apostles' Creed teaches that there is a visible communion on earth, as well as an invisible interchange of blessings between the militant and the triumphant Church,

1 Sess. XV: *". . . catholica Ecclesia . . . docuerit, purgatorium esse, animasque ibi detentas fidelium suffragiis, potissimum vero acceptabili altaris sacrificio iuvari. . . ."*

2 *" Credo sanctorum communionem."* (Apostles' Creed).

3 On the *gratia capitis* see Pohle-Preuss, *Christology,* pp. 239 sqq.

92

of which latter Purgatory is a preparatory
stage. This has always been Catholic teaching.[4]
Whereas an impassible gulf separates the
Blessed in Heaven from the demons,[5] the members of Christ's mystic body in Heaven and
on earth are closely bound together by a supernatural communion of blessings,[6] of which the
innermost essence and principle is sanctifying
grace, or theological love, and, to some extent,
theological faith. For this reason even those
Catholics who are guilty of mortal sin belong to
the militant Church and consequently, in a
restricted sense, also to the Communion of Saints.
As for the angels, they form part of the *ecclesia
triumphans,* and as such participate in the *communio sanctorum.*

Through the Communion of Saints the faithful
on earth, especially those who are in the state of
sanctifying grace, share in all the Masses, prayers, and good works offered up by the militant
Church. They are moreover benefitted by the intercession of the angels and the just in Heaven,
and they can aid the poor souls in Purgatory by prayers, indulgences, alms, and other
good works, especially by having the Sacrifice of
the Mass offered for them. The first and second
of the above-mentioned propositions having been

[4] Cfr. A. Harnack, *Apostol. Glau-
bensbekenntnis,* 9th ed., pp. 32 sqq.,
Berlin 1892.

[5] Cfr. Luke XVI, 26.
[6] Cfr. 1 Cor. XII, 24 sqq.

dealt with in previous volumes of this series,[7] it remains to prove the third, *viz.:* that the living faithful can succor the dead by works of satisfaction.[8]

2. THE DOGMA.—That the souls of the faithful departed are aided by the suffrages of the living faithful follows as a corollary from the dogma of Purgatory.[9]

Theologians are wont to quote in confirmation of this teaching certain scriptural texts, which are not, however, entirely convincing. Such a text is, *e. g.,* Tob. IV, 18: "Lay out thy bread and thy wine upon the burial of a just man, and do not eat and drink thereof with the wicked." [10] Some exegetes interpret this passage as inculcating the usefulness to the dead of a meal given to the poor in their memory.[11] But this is by no means certain. Another, equally inconclusive text often quoted in this connection is 1 Cor. XV, 29, where the Apostle speaks of persons "who are baptized for the dead." As Dr. MacRory points out, "this metaphorical sense of Baptism (as a baptism of mortification and affliction for the

---

7 Pohle-Preuss, *Mariology,* pp. 142 sqq.; *The Sacraments,* Vol. II, pp. 376 sqq.

8 On the dogma of the Communion of Saints see J. P. Kirsch, *Die Lehre von der Gemeinschaft der Heiligen im christlichen Altertum,* Mayence 1900 (tr. by J. R. McKee, *The Doctrine of the Communion of Saints in the Ancient Church; A Study in* the *History of Dogma,* London 1911); Chs. F. McGinnis, *The Communion of Saints,* St. Louis 1913.

9 *V. supra,* Sect. 1.

10 Tob. IV, 18: "*Panem tuum et vinum tuum super sepulturam iusti constitue et noli ex eo manducare et bibere cum peccatoribus.*"

11 Cfr. Bellarmine, *De Purgatorio,* I, 3.

dead) is very rare, being found only in the two passages just referred to, and there in the mouth of Christ in reference, not to ordinary mortifications, but to His baptism in His blood. This being so, is it likely that the Corinthians could be expected to think of a metaphorical baptism here? Besides, if this were the sense, the Apostle, as Estius points out, should have written, 'who baptize themselves,' *i. e.* undergo voluntary mortifications, rather than 'who are baptized.' " [12]

3. SUFFRAGES FOR THE DEAD.—In regard to suffrages for the dead (*suffragia pro mortuis*) we may ask four questions: (a) How many kinds of suffrages are there? (b) Who profits by them? (c) In what manner do they advantage the dead? and (d) By whom can they be offered?

a) There are three different kinds of suffrages by which the living can assist the dead, *viz.*: the Mass, prayers, and good works. This distinction is very old.[13]

While good works are mostly typified by alms, there are others, such as fasting, scourging, making pilgrimages, etc. The shedding of tears alone is not effective. St. Chrysostom says, " the dead are not aided by tears, but by prayer, intercession, and alms." [14]

If a man has forgotten or neglected to make restitution for some injury done to his neighbor, and others make it

12 *The Epistles of St. Paul to the Corinthians,* Part I, pp. 239 sq., Dublin 1915. Cfr. Bellarmine, *De Purg.,* I, 6.

13 *V. supra,* Sect. 1.
14 *Hom. in Ep. I. ad Cor.,* 41.

for him after his death, does he derive any spiritual benefit from the act? D. Soto [15] and Bellarmine[16] answer this question in the negative, and they are probably right. For the dead man, in omitting to make restitution, either committed a sin or he did not. If he committed a sin, he must expiate that sin, regardless of what his heirs or friends may do. If he did not sin, he incurred no punishment.

Offering up indulgences for the dead is not a distinct class of good works, because the efficacy of indulgences is conditioned upon prayer and good works. Neither are the ceremonies of Christian burial to be regarded as a special kind of suffrage, for to bury the dead is an act of corporal mercy and therefore belongs to the category of good works.[17]   The same applies to the preparation of corpses for burial, the burning of candles at the bier, sprinkling dead bodies with holy water, accompanying them to their last resting-place, decorating the graves, etc., etc.   All these are good works which help the dead if performed with the right intention.[18]

Cremation is not a good work but " a detestable abuse " in which the Church forbids Catholics to coöperate.[19] The practice of burning dead bodies, though in itself not opposed to Catholic dogma, was prohibited because it was originally introduced and is now advocated chiefly by avowed enemies of religion.[20]

---

[15] *Comment. in Sent.*, IV, dist. 45, qu. 2, art. 3.

[16] *De Purgatorio*, II, 16.

[17] Cfr. 2 Kings II, 5; Matth. XXVI. 12.

[18] Cfr. St. Thomas, *Summa Theol., Supplement.*, qu. 71, art. 11; Bellarmine, *De Purgatorio*, II, 19; L. Ruland, *Geschichte der kirchlichen Leichenfeier*, Ratisbon 1901.

[19] See the Decree of the S. Congregation of the Holy Office, of May 19, 1886.— Regarding certain conditions under which such persons may be left in good faith, see the decree of July 27, 1892, issued in reply to certain questions asked by the Archbishop of Freiburg (*Catholic Encyclopedia*, Vol. IV, p. 482).

[20] On cremation in general cfr. Wm. Devlin, *s. v.*, in the *Cath. Encyclopedia*, Vol. IV; *Acta S. Sedis*, XXV, 63; *Am. Eccles. Review*, XII, 499; *Fortnightly Review*,

b) Suffrages offered for the dead cannot benefit the just in Heaven or the damned in Hell, but they can and do benefit the poor souls in Purgatory. The just do not need human assistance. This is especially true of baptized infants and the blessed martyrs. St. Augustine says it is an insult to pray for a martyr.[21] The ancient practice, evidenced by the teaching of the Fathers and the early liturgies, of praying and offering sacrifice for deceased Apostles, martyrs, prophets, and saints, was inspired by a desire to thank God for having glorified them in Heaven. We pray for them, says St. Cyril of Jerusalem, "in order that through their prayers and supplications God may receive our own."[22] And St. Augustine: "When sacrifices . . . are offered on behalf of the very good, they are thank-offerings, . . . and in the case of the very bad, even though they do not help the dead, [these sacrifices] afford consolation to the living."[23]

c) To understand how the suffrages of the living can benefit the poor souls we must recall the distinction between the meritorious and the sat-

St. Louis, Mo., Vol. XXIII, No. 17; A. Besi, *Die Beerdigung und Verbrennung der Leichen*, Ratisbon 1889; G. Hassl, *Gottesacker oder Leichenofen*, 1898.

21 *Serm.*, 17: "*Iniuriam facit martyri, qui orat pro martyre.*" (Cfr. Pohle-Preuss, *Mariology*, p. 145).

22 *Cat. Mystag.*, V, 9: ". . . *ut Deus orationibus illorum et deprecationibus suscipiat preces nostras.*" (Migne, *P. G.*, XXXIII, 1115).

23 *Enchiridion*, 110: "*Sacrificia . . . pro valde bonis gratiarum actiones sunt; pro valde malis, si nulla adiumenta mortuorum, viventium consolationes sunt.*"

isfactory value of good works.[24]   The meritorious value of a good work consists in an increase of sanctifying grace and is not transferable. Its satisfactory value consists in an expiation of punishment due, and may be surrendered in favor of another. It is the satisfactory value alone that God accepts on behalf of the dead.

From this point of view we can appreciate the "heroic act of charity" approved by Pius IX, which consists in the voluntary relinquishment of all claim to the satisfactory fruits of one's good works as well as to the suffrages of one's friends after death for the benefit of the poor souls. However, it is doubtful whether God accepts such a sacrifice and actually deprives those who make it of the satisfactory values which they surrender. That He approves of the heroism that dictates such a noble act goes without saying, for it is in full accord with St. Paul's exclamation, "I wished myself to be an anathema from Christ, for my brethren." [25]

Over and above their meritorious and satisfactory value, prayers for the dead have an impetratory value, inasmuch as they move God to hear the petitioner's prayer, *qua* prayer, regardless of the value of the satisfaction offered.

With regard to indulgences it is commonly held that they may be applied to the poor souls "by way of suffrage" (*per modum suffragii*).[26]

d) We can offer suffrages for the dead either

24 Cfr. St. Thomas, *Summa Theol.*, Supplement., qu. 71, art. 4.

25 Rom. IX, 3: "*Optabam enim ego ipse anathema esse a Christo pro fratribus meis.*"

26 The student will find this subject treated more fully in Pohle-Preuss, *The Sacraments*, Vol. III, pp. 260 sqq.

by performing, or causing others to perform, a good work that produces its effects *ex opere operato* (*e. g.* the Mass) ; or by creating satisfactory or impetratory values for the benefit of the poor souls by giving alms, reciting the office of the dead, etc. In the former case it is sufficient that the good work be performed to secure its effects;[27] whereas in the latter case all those conditions must be fulfilled which are required to render a good work meritorious, principally this, that the applicant be in the state of sanctifying grace.[28] An act by which no merits or satisfactions are gained for the doer himself, cannot apply such merits or satisfactions to others.[29]

Can the just, who have arrived at the *status termini,* intercede for the poor souls in Purgatory?

The just who have arrived at the *status termini* are divided into two classes: (1) the Angels and Saints in Heaven, and (2) the poor souls in Purgatory.

The liturgical prayers of the Church show that the Angels and Saints, especially the Blessed Virgin Mary and St. Michael, are powerful intercessors for the dead.[30] Whether the poor souls can assist one another is a more difficult question to answer. We know that, being in a state of punishment, they all need assistance for themselves. To assume that they can obtain release

27 Cfr. Pohle-Preuss, *The Sacraments,* Vol. I, pp. 122 sqq.
28 Cfr. Pohle-Preuss, *Grace: Actual and Habitual,* pp. 82 sqq., 413.
29 Cfr. St. Thomas, *Summa Theol., Supplement.,* qu. 71, art. 3.

30 "... *ut intercedentibus omnibus Sanctis tuis pietatis tuae clementiâ omnium delictorum suorum veniam consequantur."* (Roman Missal).

from Purgatory by their own prayers, would seem to contradict the revealed teaching that they are unable to acquire merits or even quasi-merits.[31]   However, expressly excluding this untenable corollary, we may hold that the poor souls are able to pray for one another effectively. Suarez [32] and Bellarmine [33] furthermore maintain that the poor souls can aid the faithful on earth by their intercession. This is, however, opposed to the teaching of St. Thomas, who in reply to the objection that the poor souls can help us because they are friends of God says: " Those who are in Purgatory do not yet enjoy the vision of the Divine Logos, which would enable them to know what we think and speak, and therefore we do not implore their suffrages, but those of the living." [34]   The further objection that the poor souls must have power with God because they are impeccable, he refutes thus: " Though they are superior to us in as far as they can no longer sin, they are inferior to us as regards the punishments which they suffer, and therefore they are in no condition to pray [for others], but rather in a state where they need the prayers of others." [35]

Nevertheless those who piously invoke the poor souls, or promise them Masses, need not be disturbed, because it is probable that they can aid us by their intercession, and quite possible that God may aid both the poor souls and those who pray for them without the

31 On the *meritum de congruo* see Pohle-Preuss, *Grace: Actual and Habitual*, pp. 430 sqq.

32 *De Oratione*, I, 11.

33 *De Purgatorio*, II, 16.

34 *Summa Theol.*, 2a 2ae, qu. 83, art. 4, ad 3: " *Illi, qui sunt in purgatorio, nondum fruuntur visione Verbi, ut possint cognoscere ea, quae nos cogitamus vel dicimus, et ideo eorum suffragia non imploramus orando, sed a vivis petimus colloquendo.*"

35 *Op. cit.*, art. 11, ad 3: " *Illi, qui sunt in purgatorio, etsi sunt superiores nobis propter impeccabilitatem, sunt tamen inferiores quantum ad poenas, quas patiuntur, et secundum hoc non sunt in statu orandi, sed magis ut oretur pro eis.*"

knowledge of the former. Let us not forget our Saviour's dictum: "Blessed are the merciful, for they shall obtain mercy." [36] The Church in her liturgy prays *for* the poor souls, but never invokes their intercession.

READINGS: — S. J. Hunter, S.J., *Outlines of Dogmatic Theology*, Vol. III, pp. 442 sqq.— Wilhelm-Scannell, *A Manual of Catholic Theology*, Vol. II, pp. 553 sqq.— Wiseman, *Lectures on the Principal Doctrines and Practices of the Catholic Church*, Sect. XI, London 1836 (frequently reprinted).— Coleridge, *The Prisoners of the King*, London 1897.— Canty, *Purgatory, Dogmatic and Scholastic*, Dublin, 1886.— Loch, *Das Dogma der griechischen Kirche vom Purgatorium*, Ratisbon 1842.— Redner, *Das Fegefeuer*, Ratisbon 1856.— Bautz, *Das Fegefeuer*, Mayence 1883.— Tappehorn, *Das Fegefeuer*, Dillingen 1891.— St. Binet, S.J., *Der Freund der armen Seelen oder die kath. Lehre vom jenseitigen Reinigungsorte*, Freiburg 1896.— Fr. Schmid, *Das Fegefeuer nach kath. Lehre*, Brixen 1904.— IDEM, *Die Seelenläuterung im Jenseits*, Brixen 1907.— Bellarmine, *De Purgatorio.*— Casaccia, *Il Purgatorio*, Biella 1863.— B. Jungmann, *De Novissimis*, Ratisbon 1871. — Oxenham, *Catholic Eschatology*, London 1878.— Sadlier, *Purgatory: Doctrinal, Historical, Practical*, New York 1886.— Atzberger, *Geschichte der christlichen Eschatologie*, Freiburg 1896.— E. J. Hanna, art. "Purgatory," in Vol. XII of the *Catholic Encyclopedia*, pp. 375-380.— H. Thurston, S.J., *The Memory of the Dead*, London 1916 (contains a brief but fairly comprehensive sketch of the Catholic practice of prayer for the dead from the first centuries of Christianity to the close of the Middle Ages.)

36 Matth. V, 7: "*Beati misericordes, quoniam ipsi misericordiam consequentur.*"

PART II

ESCHATOLOGY OF THE HUMAN RACE

Parallel with the consummation of the individual runs the consummation of the human race, which will take place as soon as the predestined number of men is reached.

When "the last day" [1] will come no one can tell. All calculations and speculations from St. Augustine to the present have merely confirmed our Blessed Saviour's dictum that God alone knows the day and the hour when the Son of man will come to judge the living and the dead.[2]

Following St. Augustine's example [3] we shall consider, (1) the Signs that are to Precede the General Judgment, (2) the Resurrection of the Flesh, and (3) the Last Judgment.

1 John VI, 39 sq.
2 Cfr. St. Thomas, *Summa Theol.,* *Supplementum,* qu. 77, art. 2: ". . . *quorum falsitas patet et pa-* *tebit similiter eorum, qui adhuc com* *putare non cessant."*
3 *De Civitate Dei,* XX, 30.

CHAPTER I

THE SIGNS THAT ARE TO PRECEDE THE GENERAL JUDGMENT

Revelation tells us [1] that the General Judgment will be preceded by certain definite signs. Hence we may conclude that the world will not come to an end before these signs appear. On the other hand, no one can foretell the exact day of the Last Judgment from these signs. It is only when they all concur that a reasonable conjecture will become possible, and even then there will still be danger of self-deception. Cfr. 2 Thess. II, 1 sq.: "We beseech you, brethren, touching the coming of our Lord Jesus Christ and our being gathered together unto Him, that you be not readily shaken out of your right mind nor kept in alarm, —whether by spirit-utterance or by discourse or by a letter purporting to be from us,—as though the day of the Lord were upon us." [2] As the precise time of the Last Judgment is known only

1 Matth. XXIV, 37 sqq.; 2 Pet. III, 3 sqq.
2 2 Thess. II, 1 sq.: "*Rogamus autem vos fratres per adventum Domini nostri Iesu Christi, et nostrae congregationis in ipsum: ut non cito moveamini vestro sensu, neque terreamini, neque per spiritum, neque per sermonem, neque per epistolam tamquam per nos missam, quasi instet dies Domini.*"

to God, it were idle for us to speculate about it.

The principal signs or events usually enumerated by theologians as preceding the Last Judgment are:

(1) The General Preaching of the Christian Religion all over the earth;

(2) The Conversion of the Jews;

(3) The Return of Henoch and Elias;

(4) A Great Apostasy and the Reign of Antichrist;

(5) Extraordinary Disturbances of Nature;

(6) A Universal Conflagration.

1. GENERAL PREACHING OF THE CHRISTIAN RELIGION.—The first of the predicted signs was announced by our Divine Saviour Himself, Matth. XXIV, 14: "And this gospel of the kingdom shall be preached in the whole world, for a testimony to all nations, and then shall the consummation come." [3]

It must not be concluded from this prophecy that all men will ultimately embrace the Christian religion. Our Lord says that the Gospel will be preached to all nations; not that all men will be converted. [4] The words "and then" (καὶ τότε) are probably not meant to indicate an immediate sequence of events, but merely

---

[3] Matth. XXIV, 14: "Et praedicabitur hoc evangelium regni in universo orbe, in testimonium omnibus gentibus: et tunc (καὶ τότε) veniet consummatio."

[4] Cfr. St. Augustine, Ep., 199, n.

48: "In quibus gentibus nondum est Ecclesia, oportet ut sit, non ut omnes, qui ibi fuerint, credant. Omnes enim gentes promissae sunt, non omnes homines omnium gentium."

to mark the beginning (*terminus a quo*) of the period which will end with the General Judgment. "What does the phrase 'then it will come' mean," says St. Augustine, "except that it will not come before that time? How long after that time it will come, we do not know. The only thing we know for certain is that it will not come sooner." [5]

2. THE CONVERSION OF THE JEWS.—St. Paul

says: "I would not have you ignorant, brethren, of this mysery, . . . that blindness in part has happened in Israel, until the fulness of the gentiles should come in. And so all Israel should be saved, as it is written: [6] 'There shall come out of Sion he that shall deliver, and shall turn away ungodliness from Jacob.' . . . For as you also in times past did not believe God, but now have obtained mercy through their unbelief, so these also now have not believed, for your mercy, that they also may obtain mercy." [7]

From this text it may with reasonable certainty be concluded:

(a) That the majority of nations, or at least the majority of the people of all nations (*plenitudo gentium*), will embrace Christianity before the end of the world;

5 *Ep.*, 197, n. 4: "' *Tunc veniet* ' *quid est, nisi ante non veniet? Quanto post veniat, incertum nobis est. Ante tamen non esse venturum, dubitare utique non debemus.*"
6 Is. LIX, 20.
7 Rom. XI, 25 sqq.: Οὐ γὰρ θέλω ὑμᾶς ἀγνοεῖν, ἀδελφοί, τὸ μυστήριον τοῦτο, . . . ὅτι πώρωσις ἀπὸ μέρους τῷ Ἰσραὴλ γέγονεν ἄχρις οὗ τὸ

πλήρωμα τῶν ἐθνῶν εἰσέλθῃ, καὶ οὕτως πᾶς Ἰσραὴλ σωθήσεται, καθὼς γέγραπται· "Ἥξει ἐκ Σιὼν ὁ ῥυόμενος καὶ ἀποστρέψει ἀσεβείας ἀπὸ Ἰακώβ. . . . "Ωσπερ γὰρ καὶ ὑμεῖς ποτὲ ἠπειθήσατε τῷ Θεῷ, νῦν δὲ ἠλεήθητε τῇ τούτων ἀπειθείᾳ, οὕτως καὶ οὗτοι νῦν ἐπείθησαν τῷ ὑμετέρῳ ἐλέει ἵνα καὶ αὐτοὶ ἐλεηθῶσιν.

(b) That, after the general conversion of the "gentiles," the Jews, too, will accept the Gospel.

Though these propositions by no means embody articles of faith, it requires more than such antisemitic scolding as was indulged in by Luther to disprove them. The Apostle expressly speaks of a "mystery," and ascribes the final conversion of the Jews, not to the physical or mental characteristics of the Semitic race, but to a special dispensation of God's "mercy." Luther overlooked both these factors when he wrote: "A Jew, or a Jewish heart, is as hard as wood, stone, or iron, as hard in fact as the devil himself, and hence cannot be moved by any means. . . . They are young imps condemned to Hell. . . . Those who conclude from the eleventh chapter of St. Paul's Epistle to the Romans that the Jews will all be converted towards the end of the world, are foolish and their opinion is groundless." [8]

On the other hand, however, there is no reason to assume that the Jews will all be converted, or that the Hebrew race will embrace the true faith in a body. Like the "gentiles," the Jews will probably flock to the Church in great numbers. "When the multitude of nations will come in," says St. Jerome, "then this fig-tree, too, will bear fruit, and all Israel will be saved." [9]

The parable of the sheepfold (John X, 16) is sometimes applied to the end of the world, though, we believe, inaptly. In saying, "I have other sheep that are not of this fold, them also must I bring, and they shall hear

8 *Sämtl. Werke*, Jena ed., Vol. VIII, p. 109: "*Ein Jude oder jüdisch Herz ist so stock-stein-eisenteufelhart, dass mit keiner Weise zu bewegen ist. . . . Es sind junge Teufel, zur Hölle verdammt. . . . Dass etliche aus der Epistel zum Römer im 11. Kapitel solchen Wahn schöpfen, als sollten alle Juden bekehrt werden am Ende der Welt, ist nichts.*"

9 *In Habac.*, III, 17: "*Quum intraverit plenitudo gentium, tunc etiam haec ficus afferet fructus suos et omnis Israel salvabitur.*"

my voice, and there shall be one fold and one shepherd," our Lord simply meant that His Church was to embrace all nations.

3. RETURN OF HENOCH AND ELIAS.—The belief that Elias and Henoch will return to herald the second coming of our Lord and to convert the Jews, was widely held among the Fathers.

a) So far as it regards Elias, this belief is based on the prophecy of Malachias: "Behold I will send you Elias the prophet, before the coming of the great and dreadful day of the Lord. And he shall turn the heart of the fathers to the children, and the heart of the children to their fathers: lest I come and strike the earth with anathema."[10] "Elias the prophet" cannot be identical with John the Baptist, as some have thought, because the Septuagint expressly calls him "the Thesbite."[11] Moreover, our Lord Himself clearly distinguishes between the two, and ascribes to Elias precisely the rôle that was attributed to him by His contemporaries. Matth. XVII, 11 sq.: "But he answering, said to them: Elias indeed shall come, and restore all things; but I say to you that Elias is already come. . . . Then the disciples understood that he had spoken to them of John the Baptist."[12] St. Augustine explains this text as follows: "As there are two advents of the

10 Mal. IV, 5 sq.: "Ecce ego mittam vobis Eliam prophetam, antequam veniat dies Domini magnus et horribilis. Et convertet cor patrum ad filios et cor filiorum ad patres eorum, ne forte veniam et percutiam terram anathemate." (Cfr. Eccles. XLVIII, 10).

11 ὁ Θεσβίτης.
12 Matth. XVII, 11 sqq.: Ἠλείας μὲν ἔρχεται καὶ ἀποκαταστήσει πάντα· λέγω δὲ ὑμῖν ὅτι Ἠλείας ἤδη ἦλθεν. . . . Τότε συνῆκαν οἱ μαθηταὶ ὅτι περὶ Ἰωάννου τοῦ βαπτιστοῦ εἶπεν αὐτοῖς.

Judge, so there are two precursors. . . . He sent before
Him the first precursor and called him Elias, because
Elias was to take the same part in the second coming that
John had in the first." [13]
From what we have said it further appears that the
phrase " *dies Domini* " does not mean the first coming of
Christ as the Messias, but His second coming as the Uni-
versal Judge. The day of His Incarnation was a day of
mercy and blessing; the day of the Last Judgment will be
a " day of terror."

b) Concerning Henoch the argument is less
convincing.

Some theologians substitute Moses or Jeremias for
Henoch, but this procedure is rejected by the majority.[14]
The Bible says that "Henoch pleased God, and was
translated into paradise, that he may give [preach]
repentance to the nations." [15]   The Septuagint is less
definite.   It says: καὶ μετετέθη (εἰς παράδεισον is missing)
παράδειγμα μετανοίας ταῖς γενεαῖς,— which might mean that
Henoch was set up as an example of repentance for his
contemporaries.   St. Paul says: " By faith Henoch was
translated, that he should not see death." [16]   In view of
this passage and of the " two witnesses " who according to the Apocalypse (XI, 3 sqq.) will appear as precursors of our Lord when He returns for the Last Judgment, there has existed in the Church since the earliest
times a popular belief that Elias and Henoch will return

13 *Tract. in Ioa.*, VII, 5: " *Quomodo duo adventus iudicis, ita duo
praecones. . . . Misit ante se primum praeconem, vocavit illum Eliam, quia hoc erit in secundo adventu Elias, quod in primo Ioannes.*"

14 Cfr. Suarez, *De Myst. Vitae
Christi*, disp. 55, sect. 3.
15 Eccles. XLIV, 16.
16 Heb. XI, 5: " *Fide Henoch
translatus est, ne videret mortem . . .*"

to preach penance before the end of the world. However, this is not a dogmatically certain truth, as claimed by Bellarmine.[17]

4. THE GREAT APOSTASY AND ANTICHRIST.—

The "great apostasy," *i. e.* a tremendous defection among the faithful, is described partly as the cause and partly as an effect of the appearance of Antichrist. Both events may be reckoned among the signs that are to precede the Last Judgment, because it is certain that either before or after the conversion of nations and of the Jewish race there will be a great revolt, led by Antichrist, which will reduce the number of the faithful.

a) That a great apostasy will occur before the end of the world we know from St. Paul's Second Epistle to the Thessalonians.

The congregation at Thessalonica had taken alarm at a spurious letter purporting to come from the Apostle, "as though the day of the Lord were near." To prove the genuineness of the present epistle, and as a precaution against forgery, St. Paul inserts the following words in his own handwriting: "I, Paul, [send you] this greeting with my own hand. That is the sign in every letter; thus I write."[18] His references to the end of the world appear rather obscure to us because he adverts to certain things which he had told the Thessalonians by word of mouth and of which we have no knowledge: "Do you not remember that while I was still with you I used

17 *De Romano Pontifice*, III, 6.
18 2 Thess. III, 17: *"Salutatio, mea manu Pauli, quod est signum in omni epistola. Ita scribo."*

to tell you these things?"[19] On one point, however, he is quite clear, viz.: that the "day of the Lord" (ἡ ἡμέρα τοῦ κυρίου) will not come "unless the apostasy first befall, and the man of lawlessness be revealed, the son of perdition."[20] "Apostasy" (ἡ ἀποστασία, discessio) in this connection can scarcely mean a political revolution, for the whole movement is described as "a mystery of iniquity,"[21] a satanic "seduction to evil for them that are perishing, because they have not entertained the love of the truth[22] unto their salvation. And therefore God sendeth them a working of error, that they should believe that lie,[23] in order that all may be judged that have believed the truth,[24] but have acquiesced in unrighteousness."[25]

It is true that some older exegetes understood this text as foreshadowing, at least secondarily, a great political upheaval, in particular the fall of the Roman Empire.[26] But neither this catastrophe, nor the Protestant Reformation (1517), nor the dissolution of the Holy Roman Empire (1806), have proved to be the discessio predicted by the Apostle.

b) In the passage quoted above St. Paul mentions another sign among those preceding the day of the Lord, viz.: the revelation of the "man of

19 2 Thess. II, 5: "Non retinetis quod quum adhuc essem apud vos, haec dicebam vobis?"
20 2 Thess. II, 3: "Ne quis vos seducat ullo modo: quoniam nisi venerit discessio primum, et revelatus fuerit homo peccati, filius perditionis."
21 Mysterium iniquitatis, μυστήριον τῆς ἀνομίας.
22 τὴν ἀγάπην τῆς ἀληθείας.
23 τῷ ψεύδει.

24 τῇ ἀληθείᾳ.
25 τῇ ἀδικίᾳ. (2 Thess. II, 9-11).
26 St. Thomas interprets the text as follows: "Discessio primo est a fide, quia futurum erat ut fides a toto mundo reciperetur. . . . Discessio a Romano imperio debet intellegi, non solum a temporali, sed a spirituali, scil. a fide catholica Romanae Ecclesiae." (Expositio in Omnes S. Pauli Epistolas, cap. II, lect. 1).

sin," the "son of perdition," who is usually called Antichrist.

a) The name Antichrist is not found in the Epistles of St. Paul, but in 1 John II, 18, 22; IV, 3; 2 John VII. St. John speaks of "antichrists" in the plural number, but there can be no doubt that he believed in a personal Antichrist. Cfr. 1 John II, 18: "Little children, it is the last hour; and as you have heard that the Antichrist cometh, even now there are become many antichrists: whereby we know that it is the last hour." [27] This personal Antichrist is to be preceded by messengers who will prepare the way for him and inaugurate his reign. Cfr. 1 John IV, 3: "And every spirit that dissolveth Jesus, is not of God: and this is antichrist, of whom you have heard that he cometh, and he is now already in the world." The Greek text is more definite: καὶ τοῦτό ἐστι τὸ τοῦ ἀντιχρίστου [the work of Antichrist], ὃ [not ὅς] ἀκηκόατε ὅτι ἔρχεται, καὶ νῦν ἐν τῷ κόσμῳ ἐστὶν ἤδη. Evidently the Antichrist predicted by St. John is not merely a pretender, but the incarnate antithesis of our Divine Saviour, and therefore His deadly enemy. Whether "Antichrist" is merely a collective name for certain persons and tendencies, or whether it designates one particular person, a human individual of flesh and blood, cannot be concluded with certainty from the Johannine text. St. Paul, however, is positive on this point. He speaks of Antichrist as "the man of lawlessness," [28] "the son of perdition," [29] who "shall oppose and exalt himself against all that is called God" and "seat himself

---

[27] 1 Ioa. II, 18: "Filioli, novissima hora (ἐσχάτη ὥρα) est, et sicut audistis quia antichristus venit (ὅτι ὁ ἀντίχριστος ἔρχεται). Et nunc antichristi multi facti sunt, unde scimus quia novissima hora est."
[28] ὁ ἄνθρωπος τῆς ἁμαρτίας.
[29] ὁ υἱὸς τῆς ἀπωλείας.

in God's sanctuary, giving himself out as God."[30] "And then shall the lawless one[31] be revealed, whom the Lord Jesus shall slay with the breath of his mouth and bring to nought by the manifestation of his coming. But that other's coming is through Satan's working [attended] by every [kind of] feat and sign and lying wonder, and by every seduction to evil for them that are perishing."[32] This graphic description cannot be applied to a mere personification, but points to a concrete individual, and hence we may safely reject the figurative interpretation of "Antichrist," though it is not necessarily contrary to Catholic teaching.

β) It is difficult to say what St. John meant when he wrote in the same Epistle: "And now you know what keepeth him back (τὸ κατέχον), to the end that he may be revealed in his own season. For the mystery of lawlessness is already at work; only let him who now restraineth (ὁ κατέχων) be taken out of the way, and then shall the lawless one be revealed."[33] This obscure text has been variously interpreted. Most exegetes see in it a reference to some contemporaneous event. SS. Chrysostom and Jerome regarded the Roman Empire as the restraining influence (τὸ κατέχον, ὁ κατέχων). Others held that "the lawless one" is kept in check by the fact that the Gospel has not yet been preached to all nations and the Jewish people remain unconverted. Dr. Döllinger identified "the man of lawlessness" with the Emperor Nero, the κατέχων with Claudius, the "mystery of lawlessness" with Nero's intrigues to usurp the throne, and the

---

30 2 Thess. II, 3 sqq.
31 ὁ ἄνομος.
32 2 Thess. II, 8-10.
33 1 John IV, 6-7.— Cfr. 2 Thess. II, 6 sq.: Καὶ νῦν τὸ κατέχον

οἴδατε, εἰς τὸ ἀποκαλυφθῆναι αὐτὸν ἐν τῷ ἑαυτοῦ καιρῷ· Τὸ γὰρ μυστήριον ἤδη ἐνεργεῖται τῆς ἀνομίας· μόνον ὁ κατέχων ἄρτι ἕως ἐκ μέσου γένηται.

"sitting in the temple "[34] with the profanation and destruction of the Jewish temple under Titus and Vespasian.[35] Such historical parallels may be ingenious and entertaining, but in appraising them at their true value we must not overlook the fact that St. John speaks of the second coming of Christ, and that "he who restrains" this coming is most likely the devil, who is reserving his forces for the end of the world, when he will make his last and most formidable assault upon the human race through Antichrist.

Some conceive Antichrist to be an incarnate devil or a man possessed by Satan.[36] The rôle assigned to him, however, would seem to require an independent person. Such appellations as "the man of lawlessness" and "the son of perdition" sufficiently indicate that he will be a man, not an incarnate devil or an energumen.

The belief that Antichrist will be the son of a Jewish mother overshadowed by Satan[37] is pure conjecture. That he will be born in Syria or Babylonia, rule the world for three years from Jerusalem or Rome, and be deposed at the second coming of our Lord, are more or less probable surmises that have nothing to do with the dogmatic teaching of the Church.[38]

---

[34] Cfr. Dan. IX, 27.
[35] Döllinger, *Christentum und Kirche*, pp. 277 sqq.
[36] Cfr. St. Jerome, *In Dan.*, VII, 8: "*Unus de hominibus, in quo satanas inhabitaturus sit corporaliter.*"
[37] Cfr. Lactantius, *Instit.*, VI, 17: "*Oritur ex Syria, malo spiritu genitus, eversor et perditor generis humani.*"

[38] Cfr. Roncaglia, *Lezioni Sacre intorno alla Venuta, Costumi e Monarchia dell' Anticristo*, Rome 1718; A. J. Maas, S.J., art. "Antichrist," in Vol. I of the *Catholic Encyclopedia*; J. H. Newman, "The Patristic Idea of Antichrist" (*Discussions and Arguments on Various Subjects*, pp. 44-108, new impression, London 1907).

5. Extraordinary Disturbances of Nature.—The second coming of Christ will be sudden and terrifying. Matth. XXIV, 27: "As the lightning cometh out of the east, and appeareth even into the west, so shall also the coming of the Son of man be." [39] Luke XVII, 24: "As the lightning that lighteneth from under heaven, shineth unto the parts that are under heaven, so shall the Son of man be in his day." [40] Scripture clearly indicates that this event will be preceded by tremendous disturbances.

a) It is not easy to separate the eschatological part of our Lord's teaching from his references to the destruction of Jerusalem. However, there can hardly be a doubt that the following passage refers entirely to the end of the world: "And immediately after the tribulation of those days, the sun shall be darkened, and the moon shall not give her light, and the stars shall fall from heaven, and the powers of heaven shall be moved: and then shall appear the sign of the Son of man in heaven: and then shall all tribes of the earth mourn: and they shall see the Son of man coming in the clouds of heaven with much power and majesty." [41] The tribulations here described are partly material (extraordinary perturbations of nature) and partly spiritual (mental anguish suffered

---

[39] Matth. XXIV, 27: "*Sicut enim fulgur exit ab oriente, et paret usque in occidentem: ita erit et adventus Filii hominis.*"

[40] Luc. XVII, 24: "*Nam sicut fulgur coruscans de sub caelo in ea, quae sub caelo sunt, fulget: ita erit Filius hominis in die sua.*"

[41] Matth. XXIV, 29 sq.: "*Statim autem post tribulationem dierum illorum sol obscurabitur, et luna non dabit lumen suum, et stellae cadent de caelo, et virtutes caelorum commovebuntur: et tunc parebit signum Filii hominis in caelo: et tunc plangent omnes tribus terrae: et videbunt Filium hominis venientem in nubibus caeli cum virtute multa et maiestate.*"

by men). It will not do to interpret the passage figuratively. The Fathers and theologians accept our Lord's prophecy in its literal sense. Quite naturally, He employed the language of the people to whom He spoke, not the terminology of science. We know that the (fixed) stars cannot " fall from heaven." Hence the expression " powers of heaven " must apply to the atmospheric belt that surrounds the earth. We are forced to conclude that the words of the Bible refer to the earth alone and not to the planets and other astral bodies by which it is surrounded. True St. Paul says: " Every creature groaneth and travaileth in pain, even till now, and not only it, but ourselves also, who have the first fruits of the Spirit." [42] But nature, *i. e.* the material universe, expects redemption and consummation only in so far as it groans under the curse which deprived it of the blessings of Paradise. In matter of fact God cursed the earth, not its planets, nor the sun, nor the stars. Cfr. Gen. III, 17 sq.: " Cursed is the earth in thy work; . . . thorns and thistles shall it bring forth to thee." [43]

This simple and rational explanation is confirmed by what may be regarded as the most important of all Scriptural texts dealing with the consummation of the world, *viz.,* 2 Pet. III, 10: " But the day of the Lord shall come as a thief, in which the heavens shall pass away with great violence, and the elements shall be melted with heat, and the earth and the works which are in it shall be burnt up." [44] As the context shows, " heavens "

---

42 Rom. VIII, 22 sq.: " *Scimus enim quod omnis creatura (πάσῃ κτίσις) ingemiscit, et parturit usque adhuc. Non solum autem illa, sed et nos ipsi primitias spiritus habentes.*"

43 Gen. III, 17 sq.: " *Maledicta terra in opere tuo: . . . spinas et*

tribulos germinabit tibi."

44 2 Pet. III, 10: " *Adveniet autem dies Domini ut fur: in quo caeli magno impetu transient, elementa vero calore solventur, terra autem et quae in ipsa sunt opera, exurentur.*"

here means the atmosphere surrounding the earth, for the conflagration described by St. Peter is related to the deluge, " whereby the world that then was, being overflowed with water, perished; " whereas " the heavens and the earth, which now, by the same word are kept in store, [are] reserved unto fire against the day of judgment and perdition of ungodly men." [45] A comparison of the two sentences shows that the "heaven" which will be destroyed by fire is the same that helped to bring on the deluge. Hence it must be the atmosphere of our earth, of which alone, furthermore, it can be said that it " shall pass away with great violence." [46]

b) How are we to conceive "the new heavens" which Scripture predicts in connection with the "new earth" that is to be after the Last Judgment? [47] We shall hardly go astray if we picture this transformation as a restoration of the telluric atmosphere. The earth and its surrounding atmosphere will not be totally destroyed, but transformed into a paradise. It is hazardous to deduce more than this from the cryptic intimations found in various parts of the Bible. The analogy of faith as well as the geocentric conception of the universe known to have been held by the sacred writers favor the assumption that there is to be a re-created "heaven" (i. e. atmosphere) as well as a restored earth. In what manner the planets and stars are to be led to perfection,— we can hardly assume that they will continue their revolutions forever,— Revelation does not tell. The views held by the Fathers and medieval Scholastics were based on an

---

[45] 2 Pet. III, 6-7: "Per quae ille tunc mundus aquâ inundatus periit, caeli autem, qui nunc sunt, et terra eodem verbo repositi sunt, igni reservati in diem iudicii et perditionis impiorum hominum."

[46] 2 Pet. III, 10: "caeli magno impetu transient."—On the interpretation of 2 Pet. 6-10 see St. Augustine, De Civitate Dei, XX, 24.
[47] Cfr. Is. LXV, 17; LXVI, 22; Apoc. XXI, 1 sq.; 2 Pet. III, 13.

erroneous notion of the universe and cannot be regarded as an authentic exposition of the Catholic faith.

6. THE UNIVERSAL CONFLAGRATION.—The "end of the world" will be brought about by a great conflagration, which will destroy our planet and its atmosphere.

a) It is uncertain whether this catastrophe will take place before or after the General Judgment. The former view is based on the assumption that the advent of the Great Judge in the clouds of heaven [48] must coincide with the universal conflagration, and that this conflagration will not only cause the death of those who are still alive, but likewise supply for them the place of Purgatory. But this theory is open to many objections. In the first place it is improbable that the Last Judgment will be delayed until after the destruction and subsequent restoration of the earth, for how, in this hypothesis, would it be possible for the living to " hasten unto the coming of the Lord "? Moreover, it seems proper that the great conflagration should follow the Last Judgment and thus actually mark the end of the world.

b) By what means God will bring about this terrible conflagration we know not. It is neither probable nor necessary to assume that the phenomenon will be strictly miraculous. Even infidel scientists admit that there are a number of purely natural causes which may at any moment bring about the end of the world. If, for instance, the earth were to collide with a comet accompanied by a swarm of meteorites, or with some solar system other than our own, or if one of the so-called fixed stars were to

48 Mattb. XXIV, 29; 2 Pet. III, 10.

enter our planetary circle, the result would be destruction. Curiously enough the signs predicted by our Lord and by St. Peter as preceding or accompanying the end of the world coincide with the perturbations which present-day scientists say would probably ensue if the earth were hit by a comet. A well-known astronomer, Father Charles Braun, S.J., has called attention to the existence of comets which are ten thousand times larger than the earth. If such a ponderous body were to strike the earth at a speed of, say, six geographical miles per second, he says, " the result would be the same as if a compact mass of equal weight, shooting through space with the velocity of a cannon ball, would collide with the earth. No human being could live through such a catastrophe. Millions of luminous meteorites and meteors, which, as is well known, always accompany comets, would penetrate the atmosphere, and, by condensing, produce such enormous masses of cosmic dust that the sun would lose its splendor and glow with a reddish hue. Presently the head of the comet would arrive and either strike the earth and, by destroying its crust, cause the kernel of liquid fire to burst forth, or, leaving behind a large part of its coma, enter our atmosphere in the form of a frightful hurricane and start a general conflagration, which even the minerals could hardly resist, and which, within a few hours, would convert all organic structure into ashes." [49]

c) Will this universal conflagration annihilate the earth with all its inhabitants or will some organic beings survive? This question is inspired by curiosity rather than

49 J. Braun, S.J., *Kosmogonie vom Standpunkte christlicher Wissenschaft*, 3rd ed., pp. 383 sqq., Münster 1905.— On other possibilities see Epping, " Die Meteorite und ihr kosmischer Ursprung," in the *Stimmen aus Maria-Laach*, 1886, I, 290 sqq.; J. Pohle, *Die Sternenwelten und ihre Bewohner*, 6th ed., pp. 243 sqq., Cologne 1910.

dogmatic considerations.   The Scholastics generally held that no corruptible substances (*corpora mixta* = animals and plants) shall find a place on the " new earth." [50]   In point of fact we have no positive knowledge concerning this matter.   The Schoolmen claimed no greater weight for their theories than that due to the arguments which they adduced.   Their arguments in the present case are anything but conclusive.   Why should not God in his omnipotence endow mixed bodies with the same indestructibility or incorruptibility which is possessed by simple bodies (*corpora simplicia*), or recreate the animals and plants for the benefit of the race of transfigured men that is to inhabit the new earth?   St. Anselm seems to have had some such idea in mind when he wrote: " The earth which once harbored in its bosom the body of our Lord, will be like a great garden, which, having been watered by the blood of saints, will wear an imperishable garland of sweet-smelling flowers." [51]   This view has found favor with some modern theologians (Bautz and Einig), but though it is quite fascinating, we do not adopt it because it cannot be proved.

" Science," says Father Joseph Rickaby, " has sometimes dreamt of a final condition of things in which the machinery of the universe shall be completely run down, the energies of nature so dislocated as no longer to furnish any potentiality of organic life, a uniform temperature established everywhere, suns cooled, planetary revolutions stopped,— the realization in fact of the ὁμοῦ πάντα χρήματα, or universal deadlock, which was the Greek

---

[50] Among modern writers this view is held by Oswald (*Eschatologie*, 5th ed., Paderborn 1893).

[51] " *Terra, quae in gremio suo Domini corpus fovit, tota erit ut paradisus, et quia Sanctorum san-* *guine est irrigata, odoriferis floribus, rosis, violis immarcescibiliter erit perpetuo decorata.*" (Cfr. Suarez, *Comment. in S. Theol.*, III, qu. 59, art. 6, sect 3).

notion of a mindless chaos. Things may come to this final *impasse*, or they may not, science cannot tell. But there remains God's promise to re-establish (ἀνακεφαλαιώσασθαι, gather up under a new head) all things in Christ.[52] 'Hence it is said,' quotes St. Thomas: they are the last words of his book:[53] " I saw a new heaven and a new earth:[54] I will create new heavens and a new earth; and the things that were before shall not be in memory, neither shall they rise into thought; but ye shall be glad and rejoice forever."[55] 'So be it,' says Aquinas."[56]

READINGS: — J. B. Kraus, *Die Apokatastasis der unfreien Natur auf kath. Standpunkt*, Ratisbon 1850.— Houchedé, *Die Lehre vom Antichrist dargestellt nach der hl. Schrift und Tradition*, Ratisbon 1878.— A. Delattre, *Le Second Avènement de Jésus-Christ*, Louvain 1891.— J. Röhm, *Die protestantische Lehre vom Antichrist*, Hildesheim 1891.— Dornstetter, *Das endzeitliche Gottesreich nach der Prophetie*, Würzburg 1896.— Thomas, *Das Weltende nach der Lehre des Glaubens und der Wissenschaft*, Münster 1900.— Joh. Rademacher, *Der Weltuntergang*, Munich 1909.— Jungmann, *Tract. de Novissimis*, Ratisbon 1885.— Billot, *Quaestiones de Novissimis*, Rome 1903.— J. H. Newman, " The Patristical Idea of Antichrist," in *Discussions and Arguments on Various Subjects*, new impression London 1907 pp. 44–108.— A. J. Maas, S.J., art. " Antichrist," in the *Catholic Encyclopedia*, Vol. I, pp. 559–562.— Jowett " Excursus on the Man of Sin," in *Epistles of St. Paul*, London 1859.— P. Batiffol, art. " Apocatastasis," in the *Catholic Encyclopedia*, Vol. I, pp. 599 sq.

52 Eph. I, 10.
53 The *Summa contra Gentiles.*
54 Apoc. XXI, 1.

55 Is. LXV, 17 sq.
56 J. Rickaby, S.J., *God and His Creatures*, p. 419.

CHAPTER II

THE RESURRECTION OF THE FLESH

SECTION 1

REALITY OF THE RESURRECTION

1. DEFINITION.—The Resurrection of the flesh is one of the most important dogmas of the Christian religion.

St. Paul says: " If there is no resurrection of the dead, neither is Christ risen; and if Christ is not risen, vain truly is our preaching, vain too your faith." [1] The Bible employs " resurrection of the dead " [2] and " resurrection of the flesh " [3] synonymously. The latter phrase is the more significant because it emphasizes the body. The soul, of course, does not " return " to life; it is immortal.

The Resurrection of the flesh may be defined as "a substantial conversion whereby a human being, which has been resolved into its component elements by death, is restored to its former condition."

[1] 1 Cor. XV, 13 sq.: " *Si autem resurrectio mortuorum non est: neque Christus resurrexit; si autem Christus non resurrexit, inanis est ergo praedicatio nostra, inanis est et fides vestra."*

[2] *Resurrectio mortuorum* or *de mortuis,* ἀνάστασις τῶν νεκρῶν or ἐκ νεκρῶν.

[3] *Resurrectio carnis,* ἀνάστασις σαρκός.

The Resurrection is called a conversion (*mutatio*) to distinguish it from creation (*creatio ex nihilo*), by which an entirely new being comes into existence. The change involved in the Resurrection is substantial because it affects the substance of human nature, and not merely its accidents. The subject is a corruptible being, composed of elements which are separated by death and thus admit of substantial destruction. Man as such is destroyed, and of the two essential elements that compose him, *viz.*: body and soul, the former gradually returns to dust. Its resurrection is not a re-creation, but a miraculous reproduction (*reproductio*) with full identity of subject.

2. HERETICAL ERRORS VS. THE DOGMATIC TEACHING OF THE CHURCH.—The Resurrection of the dead appeared foolish to the gentiles.[4] It was denied by the Sadducees,[5] the Gnostics, the Manichæans, and the medieval Albigenses and Waldenses, and is still violently attacked by atheists, materialists, and rationalists. Against all these the Catholic Church firmly upholds the Resurrection of the body. The dogma is expressly mentioned in the so-called Apostles' Creed, in the Nicene and the Athanasian creeds, in the symbol of the Eleventh Council of Toledo, and other ancient professions of faith. Origen's teaching of an Apocatastasis of the dead[6] was condemned by the Council of Constantinople

4 Cfr. Acts XVII, 18.
5 Cfr. Matth. XXII, 23: ". . . Sadducaei, qui dicunt non esse resurrectionem."
6 V. supra, pp. 67 sqq.

(553).[7] The Fourth Council of the Lateran specifically defined that "all men will arise [from the dead] with their own proper bodies."[8]

3. PROOF FROM SACRED SCRIPTURE.—The Resurrection of the body is mentioned in both the proto- and the deutero-canonical books of the Old Testament. The former advert to it veiledly, whereas the latter inculcate it with perfect clearness.

a) The proto-canonical books contain two classes of texts referring to the Resurrection. Some predict the restoration of Israel under the figure of a general rising of the dead; others point to the Resurrection of Christ as a symbol of our own.

a) The prophet Osee puts these words into the mouths of the Jewish exiles in Babylonia: " He will revive us after two days: on the third day he will raise us up, and we shall live in his sight."[9] Yahweh Himself promises his chosen people through the same prophet: " I will deliver them out of· the hand of death. I will redeem them from death. O death, I will be thy death; O hell, I will be thy bite."[10]

Another argument may be deduced from the famous vision of Ezechiel. The prophet saw how the dry bones that lay scattered over the plain of the dead, at God's command began to stir, took on sinews and flesh, and were

---

7 " Si quis dixerit, quod in fabulosa restitutione futurae sunt solae mentes nudae, anathema sit." (Denzinger, 9th ed., n. 200).

8 " Omnes cum suis propriis resurgent corporibus." (Denzinger-Bannwart, 11th ed., n. 429).

9 Os. VI, 3: " Vivificabit nos post duos dies: in die tertia suscitabit nos, et vivemus in conspectu eius."

10 Os. XIII, 14: " De manu mortis liberabo eos, de morte redimam eos: ero mors tua o mors, morsus tuus ero inferne." (Cfr. 1 Cor. XV, 54 sq.)

covered with skin. When they stood upright, and lived
and breathed, the Lord said to the prophet: "Son of man,
all these bones are the house of Israel. . . . Behold I
will open your graves, and will bring you out of your sep-
ulchres, O my people, and will bring you into the land of
Israel." [11] Though this vision symbolizes the restoration of Israel, it would have been unintelligible to the
Jews had they not been familiar with belief in a resurrection.[12]

β) The texts of the second group refer to the
Resurrection of the Messias, which we Christians
rightly regard as a figure and pledge of our own.
Cfr. Ps. XV, 10: "Thou wilt not leave my soul
in the nether world,[13] nor wilt thou give [permit]
thy holy one to see corruption." [14]

b) A veritable *locus classicus* for the dogma of
the Resurrection is Job XIX, 23 sqq.: "Who
will grant me that my words may be written? who
will grant me that they may be marked down in
a book with an iron pen and in a plate of lead, or
else be graven with an instrument in flint stone?
For I know my Redeemer liveth, and in the last
day I shall rise out of the earth, and I shall be
clothed again with my skin, and in my flesh I shall
see my God, whom I myself shall see, and my eyes
shall behold, and not another: this my hope is laid

---

11 Ez. XXXVII, 11 sq.: "*Fili
hominis, ossa haec universa domus
Israel est. . . . Ecce ego aperiam tu-
mulos vestros et educam vos de
sepulchris vestris, populus meus:
et inducam vos in terram Israel.*"

12 Cfr. Tertullian, *De Resurrectione Carnis*, 30: "*Non posset de
ossibus figura componi, si non id
ipsum et ossibus eventurum esset.*"
13 εἰς ᾅδην; Hebrew, *sheol.*
14 Cfr. Acts II, 31 sq.; XIII, 35.

up in my bosom." [15] So clearly does this passage
express the dogma of the Resurrection that St.
Jerome says: "Job prophesied the resurrection
of the body in such plain terms that no man
has written of it more clearly or more certainly,
. . . no one [has treated this dogma] as openly
after Christ as Job did before Him." [16]

The Hebrew text, it is true, differs slightly from the
Vulgate rendering, which is followed by our English
Bible. It runs something like this: "I know that my
Redeemer liveth, and he will in the end stand above the
dust. Then shall I be clothed with this skin, and in my
flesh I shall see God. Yea, I will see him for myself,
my eyes will see him, and not another: my reins con-
sume themselves in my bosom." But, though the word-
ing is different, the hope of a glorious Resurrection is
common to both versions. Where the Vulgate says, "*Et
in novissimo die de terra resurrecturus sum,*" the Hebrew text has: "He [*i. e.* the Redeemer] will stand
above the dust." Both passages affirm the fact of the
Resurrection, with this difference, that one mentions its
efficient, while the other speaks of its formal cause. To
interpret the whole passage as merely voicing Job's
confidence of regaining his health, will not do. For in
that assumption, as even Rabbi Rosenmüller admits, there

---

15 Job XIX, 23 sqq.: "*Quis mihi
det, ut exarentur in libro stylo ferreo
et plumbi lamina vel celte sculpan-
tur in silice? Scio enim quod Re-
demptor meus vivit, et in novissimo
die de terra surrecturus sum: et rur-
sum circumdabor pelle mea, et in
carne mea videbo Deum meum, quem
visurus sum ego ipse, et oculi mei*
conspecturi sunt, et non alius: re-
posita est haec spes mea in sinu
meo.*"

16 *Ep.*, 53, 8: "*Iob resurrectionem
corporum sic prophetat, ut nullus de
ea vel manifestius vel cautius scrip-
serit, . . . nullus tam aperte post
Christum, quam iste ante Christum.*"

would be no proportion between the majestic announcement with which the text opens, and the unimportant fact which it records.[17] The logical sequence of ideas demands that Job meet the charges of his friends by expressing his belief that the due proportion between guilt and punishment will be restored in the world beyond, especially since he himself had just closed his earthly account in the sure expectation of death.[18] " We must assume," says Rosenmüller, " that his thoughts were directed to the final resurrection of the body and the restoration of all things." [19]

c) The deutero-canonical books of the Old Testament teach the doctrine of the Resurrection explicitly.

Ecclesiasticus is not entirely conclusive because the Greek text is badly corrupted and differs in many places from the Latin Vulgate. Nevertheless, the praise of Elias, who is expected to return at the end of the world, may be quoted. The Greek text says: " Blessed are they that saw thee [*i. e.* Elias at the end of the world] and were honored in love; for we too shall live." [20]

That the post-exilic Jews firmly believed in the Resurrection of the flesh is proved by the glorious martyrdom of the seven brethren and their mother, recounted in 2 Mach. VII, 9 sqq. " Thou indeed, O most wicked man," says the second of the brothers to the cruel tyrant Antiochus, " destroyest us out of this present life, but the King

---

17 Rosenmüller, *Scholia in Librum Iob, i. h. l.*
18 Iob XVII.
19 *Scholia in Librum Iob, h. l.*: " *Oportet eum de venturo iudicio, corporum resurrectione ultimâ et rerum omnium instauratione cogitasse.*"

20 Ecclus. XLVIII, 11, ed. Tischendorf, 1882: Μακάριοι οἱ ἰδόντες σε καὶ οἱ ἐν ἀγαπήσει κεκοσμημένοι· καὶ γὰρ ἡμεῖς ζωῇ ζησόμεθα.

of the world will raise us up, who die for his laws, in the resurrection of eternal life." [21]   And the fourth declares: "It is better, being put to death by men, to look for hope from God, to be raised up again by him: for, as to thee thou shalt have no resurrection unto life." [22]   The mother exhorts them all to be steadfast. "The Creator of the world," she says, ". . . will restore to you again in his mercy both breath and life." [23]   When Razias, one of the ancients of Jerusalem, was put to death for his loyalty to the Jewish religion, we are told that, "as he had yet breath in him, being inflamed in mind, he arose, and while his blood ran down with a great stream, and he was grievously wounded, he ran through the crowd, and standing upon a steep rock, when he was now almost without blood, grasping his bowels with both hands, he cast them upon the throng, calling upon the Lord of life and spirit to restore these to him again: and so he departed this life." [24]

d) In the New Testament we have the distinct assurance of Christ and His Apostles that the dead will rise again.

a) Our Lord says: "Fear ye not them that

21 2 Mach. VII, 9: "*Tu quidem scelestissime in praesenti vita nos perdis: sed Rex mundi defunctos nos pro suis legibus in aeternae vitae resurrectione suscitabit.*"

22 2 Mach. VII, 13: "*Potius est ab hominibus morti datos spem expectare a Deo, iterum ab ipso resuscitandos: tibi enim resurrectio ad vitam non erit.*"

23 2 Mach. VII, 23: "*mundi Creator et spiritum . . . vobis iterum cum misericordia reddet et vitam.*"

24 2 Mach. XIV, 46: "*. . . et quum adhuc spiraret, accensus animo, surrexit: et quum sanguis eius magno fluxu deflueret, et gravissimis vulneribus esset saucius, cursu turbam pertransiit: et stans supra quandam petram praeruptam, et iam exsanguis effectus, complexus intestina sua, utrisque manibus proiecit super turbas, invocans dominatorem vitae ac spiritus, ut haec illi iterum redderet: atque ita vitâ defunctus est.*"

kill the body, and are not able to kill the soul: but rather fear him that can destroy both soul and body in hell."[25] He accuses the Sadducees, who denied the Resurrection, of ignorance. "You err," he says, "not knowing the scriptures, nor the power of God."[26] When Martha before the tomb of her brother exclaimed, "I know that he shall rise again in the resurrection at the last day,"[27] Jesus said, "I am the resurrection and the life: he that believeth in me, although he be dead, shall live."[28] On another occasion He predicted that He Himself would raise the dead to life: "The hour cometh, wherein all that are in the graves shall hear the voice of the Son of God; and they that have done good things, shall come forth unto the resurrection of life; but they that have done evil, unto the resurrection of judgment."[29] Those who eat of the "true bread of heaven," *i. e.* His Body and Blood in the Holy Eucharist, have our Lord's solemn promise that He will "raise them up in the last day."[30]

25 Matth. X, 28: "*Nolite timere eos, qui occidunt corpus, animam autem non possunt occidere: sed potius timete eum, qui potest et animam et corpus perdere in gehennam.*"

26 Matth. XXII, 29: "*Erratis nescientes Scripturas, neque virtutem Dei.*"

27 John XI, 24: "*Scio quia resurget in resurrectione in novissimo die.*"

28 John XI, 25: *Ego sum resurrectio et vita: qui credit in me, etiam si mortuus fuerit, vivet.*"

29 John V, 28 sq.: "*. . . venit hora, in qua omnes, qui in monumentis sunt, audient vocem Filii Dei: et procedent qui bona fecerunt, in resurrectionem vitae, qui vero mala egerunt, in resurrectionem iudicii.*"

30 John VI, 40: "*Ego resuscitabo eum in novissimo die.*"

β) The Apostles testified both to the Resurrection of Christ and to the General Resurrection of the dead, with such power that the Sadducees were "grieved." [31]   St. Paul places the Resurrection of the dead on the same level, as regards certainty, with the Resurrection of our Lord: "Now if Christ is preached as risen from the dead, how say some among you that there is no resurrection of the dead? If there is no resurrection of the dead, neither is Christ risen; and if Christ is not risen, vain truly is our preaching, vain too your faith." [32]   Again he says: "If the spirit of him that raised up Jesus from the dead, dwell in you: he that raised up Jesus Christ from the dead shall quicken also your mortal bodies, because of his spirit that dwelleth in you." [33] And: "Know you not that all we who are baptized in Christ Jesus are baptized in his death? For we are buried together with him by baptism into death; that as Christ is risen from the dead by the glory of the Father, so we also may walk in newness of life." [34]   The Apostle pro-

---

[31] Acts IV, 2: "*Dolentes quod docerent populum, et annuntiarent in Iesu resurrectionem ex mortuis.*"
[32] 1 Cor. XV, 12 sqq.: "*Si autem Christus praedicatur quod resurrexit a mortuis, quomodo quidam dicunt in vobis, quoniam resurrectio mortuorum non est? Si autem resurrectio mortuorum non est, neque Christus resurrexit; si autem Christus non resurrexit, inanis est* ergo praedicatio nostra; inanis est et fides vestra."
[33] Rom. VIII, 11: "*Quod si spiritus eius, qui suscitavit Iesum a mortuis, habitat in vobis, qui suscitavit Iesum Christum a mortuis, vivificabit et mortalia corpora vestra, propter inhabitantem Spiritum eius in vobis.*"
[34] Rom. VI, 3 sqq.: "*An ignoratis quia quicunque baptizati sumus*

claimed the doctrine of the Resurrection before the Epicureans and the Stoics,[35] and courageously upheld it in the presence of Felix, the governor,[36] and King Agrippa.[37] Hymeneus and Philetus were publicly denounced by him as apostates for having taught that "the resurrection is past already."[38]

4. PROOF FROM TRADITION.—The Tradition of the early Church agrees perfectly with the teaching of the Bible. To construe a complete Patristic argument for the Resurrection, "one would have to transcribe almost all the writings of the early Fathers,"[39] for not only do they all mention the dogma occasionally, but a number of them (Athenagoras, Justin Martyr, Theophilus, Clement of Alexandria, Origen, Gregory of Nyssa, Ephraem, Tertullian, Minucius Felix, Ambrose, and others) have left special treatises on the subject.

If we study the arguments of these Fathers we find that they embody splendid proofs for the fitness of the Resurrection. Thus Minucius Felix points to the analogy

in Christo Iesu, in morte ipsius baptizati sumus? Consepulti enim sumus cum illo per baptismum in mortem: ut quomodo Christus surrexit a mortuis per gloriam Patris, ita et nos in novitate vitae ambulemus." (Cfr. 2 Cor. IV, 14; Heb. VI, 2).

35 Acts XVII, 18 sqq.
36 Acts XXIV, 15.

37 Acts XXVI, 8, 23.
38 2 Tim. II, 18: ". . . resurrectionem esse iam factam."—The Scriptural argument for the Resurrection of the dead is more fully developed by Fr. Schmid, *Der Unsterblichkeitsglaube in der Bibel,* Brixen 1902.
39 Thus Oswald, *Eschatologie,* p. 288.

existing between revelation and nature. "The sun," he says, "sinks down and rises, the stars pass away and return, the flowers die and revive again, the shrubs resume their leaves after their wintry decay, seeds do not flourish unless they are rotted. . . . So we, too, must wait for the springtime of the body."[40] The Fathers refute the objection that it is impossible for the dead to return to life by pointing to the divine omnipotence. Thus Cyril of Jerusalem says: "God created us out of nothing; why should He not be able to re-awaken that which is destroyed?"[41] St. Irenaeus emphasizes the dignity of the body as the temple of the Holy Ghost and receptacle of the Eucharistic Christ. "How can it be asserted," he asks, "that the flesh which is nourished with the Body and Blood of our Lord shall not partake of the life?"[42] St. Clement of Rome declares that the body must rise again in order to be rewarded for the merits it has acquired here below.[43] Tertullian argues that if there were no resurrection of the body, the devil would prove mightier than God and the divine economy of grace would show a fatal defect.[44]

40 *Octavius,* 34: "*Sol demergitur et nascitur, astra labuntur et redeunt, flores occidunt et reviviscunt, post senium arbusta frondescunt, semina nonnisi corrupta reviviscunt.* . . . *Expectandum nobis etiam corporis ver est.*"
41 *Catech.,* 18.
42 *Adv. Haeres.,* IV, 18: "*Quomodo dicunt, carnem non percipere vitam, qua corpore Domini et sanguine alitur?*" (Cfr. Pohle-Preuss, *The Sacraments,* Vol. II, pp. 71 sq.).
43 *Ep. ad Corinth.,* I, 25: καὶ

ἀναστήσεις τὴν σάρκα μου ταύτην τὴν ἀνατλήσασαν ταῦτα πάντα.
44 *De Resurrectione Carnis,* c. 46: "*Diabolus validior in hominem intellegitur totum eum elidens, Deus infirmior renuntiabitur non totum relevans. Atqui et Apostolus suggerit, ubi delictum abundaverit, illic gratiam abundasse.*" — Cfr. G. Scheurer, *Das Auferstehungsdogma der vornizänischen Zeit,* Würzburg 1896; H. Kihn, *Patrologie,* Vol. I, pp. 172 sqq., 289 sqq.; Vol. II, pp. 160, 470 et passim, Paderborn 1904-1908.

SECTION 2

UNIVERSALITY OF THE RESURRECTION

1. The Catholic Church teaches that on the Last Day all men shall rise in the flesh,—the just to be rewarded with eternal life, the wicked to be punished with eternal death.

Though the early creeds stress the fate of the just,[1] the Church has never permitted her children to doubt that the wicked also will rise in the flesh. The so-called Athanasian Creed says: "All men shall rise again with their bodies, and shall give an account of their works; and they that have done good shall go into life everlasting, and they that have done evil, into everlasting fire." [2]

The Fourth Council of the Lateran defines: "All men shall rise again with their own bodies, which they now have, to receive according to their deeds, whether good or bad: the latter, everlasting punishment with the devil, the former, eternal glory with the Lord." [3]   Hence it is an ar-

---

1 Cfr. the *Symbolum Nicaenum* as revised at Constantinople: "*Et expecto resurrectionem mortuorum et vitam venturi saeculi.*"

2 " *Omnes homines resurgere habent* [i. e. *resurgent*] *cum corpori-* bus suis, *etc.*" (Denzinger-Bannwart, n. 40).

3 " *Omnes cum suis propriis resurgent corporibus, quae nunc gestant, ut recipiant secundum opera 'sua, sive bona fuerint sive mala: illi*

132

ticle of faith that the souls of the damned as well as those of the Elect will be reunited to their bodies on the last day.

a) This teaching can be convincingly demonstrated from Holy Scripture. Cfr. Dan. XII, 2: "And many of those that sleep in the dust of the earth shall awake: some unto life everlasting, and others unto reproach, to see it always." [4] Our Lord Himself says: "They that have done good things shall come forth unto the resurrection of life; but they that have done evil, unto the resurrection of judgment." [5] St. John writes in the Apocalypse: "And the dead were judged by those things which were written in the books, according to their works. And the sea gave up the dead that were in it, and death and hell gave up their dead that were in them; and they were judged every one according to their works. And hell and death were cast into the pool of fire. This is the second death. And whosoever was not found written in the book of life, was cast into the pool of fire." [6] St. Paul, when brought

cum diabolo poenam perpetuam, et isti cum Christo gloriam sempiternam." (Denzinger-Bannwart, n. 429).

[4] Dan. XII, 2: "Et multi de his, qui dormiunt in terrae pulvere, evigilabunt: alii in vitam aeternam, et alii in opprobrium ut videant semper."

[5] Ioa. V, 29: "Procedent qui bona fecerunt, in resurrectionem vitae: qui vero mala egerunt in resurrectionem iudicii."

[6] Apoc. XX, 12 sqq.: ". . . et iudicati sunt mortui ex his, quae scripta erant in libris secundum opera ipsorum. Et dedit mare mortuos, qui in eo erant: et mors et infernus dederunt mortuos suos, qui in ipsis erant: et iudicatum est de singulis secundum opera ipsorum. Et infernus et mors missi sunt in stag-

before Felix, the governor, openly professed his belief in "a resurrection of the just and the unjust." [7]

A difficulty has been raised in view of Ps. I, 5: " Therefore the wicked shall not rise again in judgment." [8] But this difficulty is apparent rather than real. The Royal Psalmist does not except the wicked from the General Resurrection; he merely wishes to say that they will be unable to stand judgment. This is clearly apparent from the Hebrew text, which says: " The wicked shall not stand, but be as dust which the wind driveth from the face of the earth."

b) Though the Fathers devote more attention to the Resurrection of the just, there can be no reasonable doubt that they believed also in the Resurrection of the wicked.

Clement of Rome admonishes the Corinthians : " Keep the flesh pure and the seal undefiled, that we may obtain eternal life, and let none of you say that this flesh is not judged and does not rise again." [9] His meaning evidently is that impurity will be punished, as purity is rewarded, in the flesh. Tertullian testifies to the early belief in Christ's return to judge the wicked and the just, rewarding the latter with eternal life and punishing the

num ignis."—On the "Book of Life" see Pohle-Preuss, Grace, Actual and Habitual, pp. 192 sq.

7 Acts XXIV, 15: ". . . resurrectionem futuram iustorum et iniquorum (δικαίων τε καὶ ἀδίκων)."

8 Ps. I, 5: "Ideo non resurgent impii in iudicio."

9 II Ep. ad Corinth., 8, 6-9, 1: τηρήσατε τὴν σάρκα ἁγνὴν καὶ τὴν σφραγῖδα ἄσπιλον, ἵνα τὴν αἰώνιον ζωὴν ἀπολάβωμεν καὶ μὴ λεγέτω τις ὑμῶν, ὅτι αὕτη ἡ σάρξ οὐ κρίνεται οὐδὲ ἀνίσταται.

former with eternal fire, after they have all arisen from the dead and resumed their bodies.[10]

c) Though reason cannot prove the necessity of the Resurrection, it can show its congruity.

" It is against the nature of the soul," says St. Thomas, " to be without the body. But nothing that is against nature can be lasting. Therefore the soul will not be forever without the body. Thus the immortality of the soul seems to require the resurrection of the body." [11] However, this argument must not be strained. It does *not* prove the impossibility of an eternal separation between body and soul. If it did, a natural resurrection of the flesh would have to be postulated for the pure state of nature, and the dogma of the Resurrection could be conclusively proved from philosophy. Some Catholic writers have indeed asserted this to be so.[12] Scheeben shatters their arguments by showing the essentially supernatural character of the Resurrection.[13] Man has no natural claim to be restored to life after death, least of all in a transfigured body, and to say that God might allow the souls of the dead to live forever without their bodies involves no contradiction, either against the order

10 *De Praescript.*, 13: " *Credimus . . . Christum venturum cum claritate ad iudicandos sanctos in vitae aeternae et promissorum caelestium fructum, et ad profanos adiudicandos igni aeterno factâ utrisque partis resurrectione cum restitutione carnis.*"

11 *Summa contra Gentiles*, IV, 79: " *Est contra naturam animae absque corpore esse. Nihil autem, quod est contra naturam, potest esse perpetuum. Non igitur perpetuo erit anima absque corpore. Quum igitur per-* *petuo maneat [quia immortalis], oportet eam corpori iterato coniungere, quod est resurgere.*"— Cfr. Rickaby, *God and His Creatures*, p. 403.

12 Notably A. Feretti (*Philosophia Moralis*, pp. 88 sqq., Rome 1887) and Costa-Rossetti (*Philosophia Moralis*, 2nd ed., pp. 41 sq., Innsbruck 1886).

13 *Die Mysterien des Christentums*, 3rd ed., pp. 591 sqq., Freiburg 1912.

of nature or against any divine attribute.[14] The souls of the Old Testament patriarchs have been living without their bodies for several thousand years and will continue in a disembodied state until the day of Judgment. There is no reason for assuming that they could not exist in this way forever.

A second argument for the congruity of the Resurrection is derived from the attribute of divine justice and may be tersely formulated as follows: " Reward and punishment are due to men both in soul and body. But in this life they cannot attain to the reward of final happiness, and sins often go unpunished: nay, here 'the wicked live, and are comforted and set up with riches' (Job XXI, 7). There must, then, be a second union of soul and body, that man may be rewarded and punished in both." [15]

2. In conclusion we may add a few words concerning the raising of Lazarus and other dead persons by Christ during His earthly sojourn, and similar miracles performed by Saints. The persons thus miraculously raised were restored to life only to die again, and now await their final resurrection with the remainder of humanity.

Some doubt exists with regard to the saints who came forth bodily from their graves at the death of our Saviour.[16] There have been theologians who thought that these privileged persons anticipated, as it were, the General Resurrection and ascended to Heaven with Christ; others (e. g. Theodoret and St. Augustine) hold the more

---

14 Cfr. St. Thomas, *Summa Theol.*, *Supplement.*, qu. 75, art. 3.

15 St. Thomas, *Summa contra Gentiles*, IV, 79: " *Necessarium est, ponere iteratam ad corpus coniunctionem, ut homo in corpore et anima praemiari et puniri possit.*"

16 Cfr. Matth. XXVII, 52 sq.: " *Monumenta aperta sunt et multa corpora sanctorum, qui dormierant, surrexerunt; et exeuntes de monumentis post resurrectionem eius, venerunt in sanctam civitatem et apparuerunt multis.*"

probable opinion that they were revived only for a time and died again.   This latter theory is preferable to the former because it agrees with the Catholic belief that the bodily Assumption of the Blessed Virgin Mary is an altogether unique privilege.[17]

17 See Pohle-Preuss, *Mariology*, pp, 105 sqq.

SECTION 3

NATURE OF THE RISEN BODY

The body that will be reunited to the soul at the Resurrection will be identical with the one inhabited by the soul on earth.

1. PROOF FROM REVELATION.—The Eleventh Council of Toledo says: "We believe that we shall arise, clothed not in air or some other flesh, but in the self-same [flesh] in which we [now] live, exist, and move." [1] The so-called Creed of Leo IX, which is still employed in the consecration rite of bishops, contains this passage: "I believe also in the true resurrection of the same flesh which I now have." [2] The Fourth Council of the Lateran defines: "All men will rise again with their own bodies [the same] which they now have." [3]

a) The Biblical argument for this dogma is based on the same texts that prove the Resur-

[1] "*Nec in aëra vel qualibet alia carne, ut quidam delirant, surrecturos nos credimus, sed in ista, qua vivimus, consistimus et movemur.*" (Denzinger-Bannwart, n. 287).
[2] "*Credo etiam veram resurrectionem eiusdem carnis, quam nunc gesto.*" (Denzinger-Bannwart, n. 347).
[3] "*Omnes cum suis propriis resurgent corporibus, quae nunc gestant.*" (Denzinger-Bannwart, n. 429).

rection, especially the vision of Ezechiel and the passage from Job which we have quoted above.[4]

Where Sacred Scripture does not expressly assert the identity of the risen body with that inhabited by the soul before death, it takes this identity for granted. For a man to rise again in a strange body would not be a true resurrection. " We cannot speak of a resurrection," says St. Thomas, "unless the soul returns to the same body, because resurrection signifies *a new rising*. To rise and to fall belong to the same subject, . . . and hence, if the soul did not resume the same body, there would be no resurrection, but rather the assumption of a new body."[5]   St. Paul writes: " For this corruptible [body] must needs put on incorruption, and this mortal [body] immortality."[6]   Consequently, it is one and the same body which, having been corruptible and mortal in this life, becomes incorruptible and immortal after the Resurrection.

b) The Fathers conceived the Resurrection of the flesh as a reawakening or restoration of the body formerly inhabited by the soul, and rejected the contrary teaching of the Origenists. St. Jerome says: "As Christ arose in that body which lay with us in the sacred sepulchre, so we, on the day of judgment, shall arise in the same

4 *V. supra*, Sect. 1.

5 *Summa Theol., Supplement.*, qu. 79, art. 1: " *Non enim resurrectio dici potest, nisi anima ad idem corpus redeat, quia resurrectio est iterata surrectio. Eiusdem autem est surgere et cadere, . . . et ita, si non est idem corpus, quod anima resumit, non dicitur resurrectio, sed magis novi corporis assumptio.*"

6 1 Cor. XV, 53: " *Oportet enim corruptible hoc* (τὸ φθαρτὸν τοῦτο) *induere incorruptionem et mortale hoc* (τὸ θνητὸν τοῦτο) *induere immortalitatem.*"

bodies by which we are covered and with which we are buried."[7]   The Patristic teaching that holy Communion is a pledge of the Resurrection would be meaningless if the risen body were not identical with the one we have on earth.

Tradition expressed itself practically in the solemn burial rite of the Church, the liturgical prayers recited for the dead, the respect shown to corpses, and especially the veneration exhibited towards the bodies of saints and their relics.[8]

2. SPECULATIVE DISCUSSION OF THE DOGMA. —Speculative theology strives to understand the import of the dogma and to answer some of the questions that arise concerning the identity and integrity of the risen body and its functions.

a) As regards the *identity* of the risen body, it must be taken neither in too broad nor in too narrow a sense.

Durandus declared that identity of soul is sufficient to constitute identity of person, and that the risen body may be composed of matter entirely different from that which constituted it during life.   But would an entirely new body be really and truly " my body "?   If my soul were to inhabit an entirely new body, should I not, on the contrary, be a different person, at least materially?   The Church

---

[7] *Ep.*, 61: " *Sicut surrexit Dominus in corpore, quod apud nos in sacro sepulcro conditum iacuit, ita et nos in ipsis corporibus, quibus circumdamur et sepelimur, in die iudicii surrecturi sumus.*"

[8] Cfr.   Pohle-Preuss, *Mariology*, pp. 153 sqq.— The argument from the monuments of the early Church is well developed by Katschthaler, *Eschatologia*, pp. 448 sqq., Ratisbon 1888.

declares that after the Resurrection man will not only be of the same species as before, but identically the same individual. It makes no difference whether this identity is conceived in accordance with the hylomorphic system of Aristotle and St. Thomas, or the modern atomic theory, as long as the reality of matter is admitted. Nor, again, must the identity of the risen body be conceived too narrowly. Of course, corporeal individuality is not to be gauged by a mathematical standard. Infants and old men will probably not arise exactly as they died, but in a more perfect form. Moreover, we know that in consequence of the process technically called metabolism, the human body changes its material composition every seven years or so. Hence there can be no absolute bodily identity even in this life. Nor need the identity of the risen with the earthly body be conceived as absolute. " What does not bar numerical unity in a man while he lives on uninterruptedly," says St. Thomas, " clearly can be no bar to the identity of the risen man with the man that was. In a man's body while he lives, there are not always the same parts in respect of matter, but only in respect of species. In respect of matter there is a flux and reflux of parts: still that fact does not bar the man's numerical unity from the beginning to the end of his life." [9]

It has been objected that, as the same matter enters successively into the composition of different men, many individuals, especially savages addicted to anthropophagy, will have to fight for their bodies at the Resurrection. But

[9] *Summa contra Gentiles*, IV, 81: " *Quod non impedit unitatem secundum numerum in homine, dum continue vivit, manifestum est quod non potest impedire unitatem resurgentis. In corpore autem hominis, quamdiu vivit, non semper sunt eaedem partes secundum materiam, sed solum secundum speciem. Secundum vero materiam partes fluunt et refluunt, nec propter hoc impeditur, quin homo sit unus numero a principio vitae usque in finem.*"

this objection is unworthy of serious consideration. God
in His omnipotence and wisdom can surely find ways and
means of restoring to every man his own body.[10]

b) The *integrity* of the risen body offers a real
difficulty, owing to the fact that many men are
mutilated before they die, while others (*monstra*)
never enjoy the possession of a normal physique.

St. Augustine says on this subject: " As the members
appertain to the integrity of human nature, they shall
all be restored together; for they who were either blind
from birth, or who lost their sight on account of some disease, the lame, the maimed, and the paralyzed, shall rise
again with an entire and perfect body." [11] The same
holy Doctor expresses the expectation that " whatever
old age or disease has wasted in the body . . . shall be re-
paired by the divine power of Christ," [12] and that the
body will be raised, not in an immature or decrepit condition, but as it appeared in the prime of life.[13] However, these are mere conjectures. We have no positive
knowledge whatever on the subject.

Certain theologians hold that the bodies of the risen
will be either asexual or all of the male gender. This
opinion is untenable for the reason that the distinction of
sex appertains both to the integrity and the identity of the
individual [14] and also because our Lord seems to take the

---

10 Cfr. St. Thomas, *Summa contra Gentiles*, IV, 81.
11 *Enchiridion*, c. 89: " *Quoniam membra ad veritatem humanae
naturae pertinent, simul restituentur
omnia. Qui enim vel ab ipso ortu
oculis capti sunt vel ob aliquem mor-
bum lumina amiserunt, claudi atque*
*omnino manci et quibusvis membris
debiles integro ac perfecto corpore
resurgent."* This teaching was embodied in the Catechism of the
Council of Trent, P. I, c. 12, n. 9.
12 *De Civitate Dei*, XXII, 19.
13 *Ibid.*, XXII, 16.
14 Cfr. Gen. I, 27, 31.

continued existence of sex for granted when He says: "In the resurrection they shall neither marry nor be married."[15] In Eph. IV, 13: "Until we all meet and attain to the unity of faith, and knowledge of the Son of God, even to a perfect man, to the measure of the full stature of Christ,"[16] the context shows that the Apostle means that perfect manhood which the soul is destined to attain in the life beyond. He does *not* mean, as St. Thomas notes, that when the risen go forth to meet Christ, they shall all be of the male sex, but merely desires to foreshadow the perfection and strength of the Church, which shall be like that of a full-grown man.[17]

c) Of the bodily functions all those that pertain to the vegetative life will cease in the next world.

Nutrition and propagation are incompatible with the *status termini*. Moreover, Christ Himself expressly repudiated the idea of a Mohammedan paradise. Cfr. Matth. XXII, 30: "In the resurrection they shall neither marry nor be married, but shall be as the angels of God in heaven,"[18] that is to say, though the distinction of sex remains, its functions will cease.

Scripture often likens Heaven to a banquet, at which all men will sit down to feast with the Patriarchs. This is a mere allegory, designed to illustrate the happiness of the Elect. St. Paul says: "Food is for the belly,

15 Matth. XXII, 30: "*In resurrectione enim neque nubent, neque nubentur . . .*"

16 Eph. IV, 13: "*Donec occurramus omnes in unitatem fidei, et agnitionis Filii Dei in virum perfectum* (εἰς ἄνδρα τέλειον) *in mensu-*ram aetatis plenitudinis Christi."

17 *Summa contra Gentiles*, IV, 88.

18 Matth. XXII, 30: "*In resurrectione enim neque nubent* (γαμοῦσιν), *neque nubentur* (γαμίζονται): *sed erunt sicut angeli Dei in caelo.*"

and the belly for food; still, God will end both the one and the other." [19] This cannot mean that the organs of digestion and assimilation will be destroyed, for they belong to the integrity of the body,— but that they will no longer exercise their functions.

As regards the senses, the eyes and ears will no doubt continue to exercise their functions, the former by enjoying the sight of the God-man, the Blessed Virgin Mary, and the Saints, the latter by listening to the conversation of the Blessed and drinking in their paeans of praise and exultation. [20] What some theologians say concerning delicious odors, essences, etc., enjoyed by the Elect is pure speculation with no basis in fact.

3. THE FOUR TRANSCENDENT ENDOWMENTS OR QUALITIES OF THE RISEN BODIES OF THE SAINTS.—In addition to the natural characteristics of identity and integrity common to all risen bodies, the glorified bodies of the Elect will enjoy four supernatural qualities, *viz.:* impassibility, brightness, agility, and subtility.

a) Impassibility (*impassibilitas,* ἀφθαρσία) puts the bodies of the Elect beyond the reach of death, pain, and discomfort. 1 Cor. XV, 53: "This mortal body must needs put on incorruption." [21] Apoc. XXI, 4: "God shall wipe away every tear from their eyes, and death shall be no more,

19 1 Cor. VI, 13: "*Esca ventri et venter escis, Deus autem et hunc et has destruet."*
20 Cfr. Lessius, *De Summo Bono,* III, n. 100.

21 1 Cor. XV, 53: δεῖ γὰρ τὸ φθαρτὸν τοῦτο ἐνδύσασθαι ἀφθαρ σίαν.

neither shall mourning or wailing or pain be any more, because the first things are passed away." [22]

The term ἀφθαρσία, as employed by St. Paul, signifies something more than "incorruption." The bodies of the wicked, too, are after a fashion "incorruptible," but they are by no means impassible. Impassibility is a peculiarity of the *glorified* body. Whether it is a positive quality imparted to the soul by God, or results from the expulsion of the active and passive factors responsible for pain and suffering, we are unable to say. All that we know for certain is that the bodies of the Saints will be incapable of suffering. St. Thomas ascribes this supernatural impassibility to the complete and perfect dominion exercised by the soul over the body, whereby the latter is effectively protected against all harmful influences both from within and without.[23]

b) The second quality of the glorified body is a certain brightness (*claritas*, δόξα) that will cause the just, in the words of our Saviour Himself, to "shine as the sun." [24]

This prerogative was foreshadowed in the transfiguration of Christ on Mount Thabor. "Our conversation," says St. Paul, "is in heaven, from whence also we look for the Saviour, our Lord Jesus Christ, who will transform the body of our lowliness, that it may be one with the body of his glory, by the force of that power whereby

22 Apoc. XXI, 4: καὶ ἐξαλείψει ὁ θεὸς πᾶν δάκρυον ἀπὸ τῶν ὀφθαλμῶν αὐτῶν, καὶ ὁ θάνατος οὐκ ἔσται ἔτι, οὔτε πένθος οὔτε κραυγὴ οὔτε πόνος οὐκ ἔσται ἔτι, ὅτι τὰ πρῶτα ἀπῆλθεν.

23 *Summa Theol., Supplement.*, qu. 82, art. 1.

24 Matth. XIII, 43: "*Tunc iusti fulgebunt sicut sol in regno Patris eorum.*"

he is able to subject all things to himself." [25] Elsewhere the Apostle intimates that the body will be transfigured in proportion to the light of glory which illumines the soul and enables it to behold the divine essence. Cfr. 1 Cor. XV, 40 sq.: "The glory of the heavenly is different from that of the earthly. There is the glory of the sun, and the glory of the moon, and the glory of the stars; for star differeth from star in glory. And so it is with the resurrection of the dead." [26] "Thus," explains St. Thomas, "the glory of the soul shall be perceptible in the glorified body as the color of a body enclosed in a glass receptacle is visible through the glass." [27] As the wounds of our Divine Saviour do not disfigure His glorified body, but shine forth with indescribable radiance, so, we may assume, the scars of the blessed martyrs, far from marring, will rather enhance the beauty and glory of their transfigured bodies. [28]

c) The third quality of the glorified body is a certain agility (*agilitas*, δύναμις), by which, under the influence of the spirit, now no longer restrained, the body is freed from its innate clumsiness and moves with the utmost facility in whatever direction it is drawn by the soul.

[25] Phil. III, 20 sq.: "*Nostra autem conversatio in caelis est: unde etiam Salvatorem expectamus Dominum nostrum Iesum Christum, qui reformabit corpus humilitatis nostrae, configuratum corpori claritatis suae, secundum operationem, qua etiam possit subiicere sibi omnia.*"
[26] 1 Cor. XV, 40 sq.: ". . . *alia quidem caelestium gloria, alia autem terrestrium: alia claritas solis, alia claritas lunae, et alia claritas stellarum. Stella enim a stella differt in claritate: sic et resurrectio mortuorum.*"
[27] *Summa Theol., Supplement.*, qu. 85, art. 1: "*Et ita in corpore glorioso cognoscetur gloria animae, sicut in vitro cognoscitur color corporis, quod continetur in vase vitreo.*"
[28] Cfr. St. Thomas, *Supplement.*, qu. 82, art. 1, ad 5.

The body of our Lord after the Resurrection was no longer subject to the limitations of space. Similarly the transfigured bodies of the Saints will be able to move from place to place, from planet to planet, from star to star, with the utmost ease and celerity. St. Thomas ascribes this ability to the fact that in the glorified body the soul is free to exercise its functions as the substantial form and motive power (*vis motrix*).[29]

Can the Blessed move from place to place in a timeless moment, that is, without passing through the intervening space? This purely philosophical question is answered negatively by the Angelic Doctor. "The glorified body," he says, "moves in time, but imperceptibly because of its quickness."[30] Suarez[31] takes the opposite view and supports it with certain utterances of the Fathers. The metaphysical possibility of such unhampered motion depends on the nature of time and space.

d) The fourth and last quality of the transfigured body is subtility (*subtilitas s. spiritualitas*). This property does not imply that the glorified body (σῶμα πνευματικόν) is imperceptible to the senses, or that it is transformed into spirit.[32] The body merely enters into the full possession of grace and participates in the higher life of the soul to such an extent that it may be said to be almost spiritualized.

The soul is filled with the divine *pneuma*, which, as the principle of supernatural life, assumes into itself the

29 *Op. cit.*, qu. 84, art. 1.
30 *Ibid.*: "*Corpus gloriosum movetur in tempore, sed imperceptibiliter propter brevitatem.*"

31 *De Myst. Vitae Christi*, disp. 48, sect. 4.
32 Cfr. St. Thomas, *Summa Theol.*, Supplement., qu. 83, art. 6.

life of the body and raises it to its own level. The soul is no longer subject to death and suffering and no longer depends on material objects for the processes of nourishment and acquiring knowledge. The body becomes absolutely subject to the spirit, and the former conflict between the two is at an end.

It is a controverted question whether the transfigured bodies of the Blessed, by virtue of this supernatural gift of subtility, can penetrate one another, *i. e.* occupy the same space. Most authors hold that they are endowed with mechanical *compenetrabilitas, i. e.* the capability of mutual penetration. That this is metaphysically possible we know from the fact that Christ after the Resurrection passed through the walls of the sepulchre and the closed doors of the council chamber without let or hindrance. St. Thomas ascribes this prerogative to a special act of divine omnipotence,[33] whereas Suarez [34] thinks it may be explained as a natural effect of the spirituality of the transfigured body.

READINGS : — E. Ramers, *Des Origenes Lehre von der Auferstehung des Fleisches,* Treves 1851.— M. Seisenberger, *Die Lehre von der Auferstehung des Fleisches,* Ratisbon 1867.— J. Bautz, *Die Lehre vom Auferstehungsleibe nach ihrer positiven und spekulativen Seite,* Mayence 1877.— G. Scheurer, *Das Auferstehungsdogma der vornizänischen Zeit,* Würzburg 1896.— A. Brinquant, *La Résurrection de la Chair et les Qualités du Corps des Élus,* Paris 1899.—* F. Schmid, *Der Unsterblichkeits- und Auferstehungsglaube in der Bibel,* Brixen 1902.— Chadouard, *La Philosophie du Dogme de la Résurrection de la Chair au 2e Siècle,* Paris 1905.— A. J. Maas, S.J., art. "Resurrection," in the *Catholic Encyclopedia,* Vol. XII, pp. 792 sq.

33 Cfr. St. Thomas, *op. cit.,* qu. 83, art. 2: "*Corpus gloriosum ratione suae subtilitatis non habebit, quod possit esse simul cum alio corpore, sed poterit simul cum alio corpore esse ex operatione virtutis divinae.*"

34 *De Myst. Vitae Christi,* disp. 48, sect. 5, n. 16.

CHAPTER III

SECTION I

REALITY OF THE LAST JUDGMENT

1. THE DOGMA IN SACRED SCRIPTURE AND TRADITION.—Aside from the great conflagration which is to destroy the earth, the General Judgment (*iudicium universale*) will be the last important event in the history of the human race. This event is so intimately connected with the Resurrection of the dead, that no room remains for a terrestrial reign of Christ and His saints (*millennium*) which, the Chiliasts hold, is to precede the end of the world. That there will be a General Judgment, and that it will be held by Christ in person, has always been an article of faith in the Catholic Church, as may be seen from the ancient creeds. The Apostles' Creed expresses this belief in the words: "From whence He [Christ] shall come, to judge the living and the dead."

a) Few truths are more clearly and insistently

proclaimed in Scripture than this. The New Testament in particular speaks time and again of the "second coming" of Christ as the Universal Judge, in opposition to His "first coming" as the Redeemer. This "second coming" is commonly called *parousia, i. e.* advent;[1] sometimes "epiphany" (ἐπιφάνεια), *i. e.* apparition,[2] and sometimes "apocalypse" (ἀποκάλυψις), *i. e.* revelation.[3] Our Lord Himself predicted the General Judgment,[4] and the Apostles echoed His teaching. We have already quoted St. Paul. St. James says: "Be patient, therefore, brethren, until the coming of the Lord. . . . Grudge not one against another, that you may not be judged. Behold, the Judge standeth before the door."[5] St. Peter writes: "But the day of the Lord shall come as a thief; . . . what manner of people ought you to be in holy conversation and godliness, looking for and hasting unto the coming of the Lord, by which the heavens being on fire shall be dissolved, and the elements shall melt with burning heat."[6]

b) Though the writings of the Apostolic Fa-

[1] 1 Cor. XV, 23; 1 Thess. II, 19, and elsewhere.

[2] 2 Thess. II, 8; 1 Tim. VI, 14; 2 Tim. IV, 1; Tit. II, 13.

[3] 2 Thess. I, 7; 1 Pet. IV, 13.

[4] Matth. XXIV, 27 sqq.; XXV, 31 sqq.

[5] Iac. V, 7 sqq.: "*Patientes igitur estote fratres usque ad adventum Domini. . . . Nolite ingemiscere fratres in alterutrum, ut non iudicemini.*

Ecce iudex ante ianuam assistit."

[6] 2 Pet. III, 10 sqq.: "*Adveniet autem dies Domini ut fur: . . . quales oportet vos esse in sanctis conversationibus et pietatibus, expectantes et properantes in adventum diei Domini, per quem caeli ardentes solventur, et elementa ignis ardore tabescent?*" Cfr. Apoc. XX, 11 sqq.; additional scriptural texts infra, No. 2.

thers are tinged with Chiliastic views,[7] the dogma of the Last Judgment has a solid Patristical foundation. Clement of Rome refers to Christ as "judge of the living and the dead." [8] In the so-called Epistle of Barnabas we read that the Son of God is "destined to judge the living and the dead." [9] Tertullian writes: "Christ will return on the clouds of heaven, the same as He arose." [10]

2. ATTENDING CIRCUMSTANCES OF THE GENERAL JUDGMENT.—Sacred Scripture expressly mentions certain features of the General Judgment.

a) Our Lord Jesus Christ will conduct the trial in person. John V, 22: "The Father . . . hath given all judgment to the Son." [11] He will be assisted by the angels. Matth. XXIV, 31: "[The Son of man] shall send his angels with a trumpet and a great voice, and they shall gather together his elect from the four winds, from the farthest parts of the heavens to the utmost bounds of them." [12]

b) The site of the Last Judgment, according to the prophet Joel, will be the valley of Josaphat.[13] St. Paul

7 V. infra, Sect. 2.

8 κριτοῦ ζώντων καὶ νεκρῶν. (Epist. ad Corinth., I, 2, 1).

9 μέλλων κρίνειν ζῶντας καὶ νεκρούς. (Ep. Barnab., VII, 1).

10 Adv. Prax., c. 30: "Christus venturus est rursus super nubes caeli, qualis et ascendit."

11 Ioa. V, 22: "Pater . . . omne iudicium dedit Filio."

12 Matth. XXIV, 31: "Et mittet angelos suos cum tuba et voce magna, et congregabunt electos eius a quattuor ventis, a summis caelorum usque ad terminos eorum." (Cfr. 1 Cor. XV, 52; 1 Thess. IV, 15).

13 Joel III, 2: "Congregabo omnes gentes et deducam eas in vallem Iosaphat."— Cath. Encycl., Vol. VIII, p. 503

says the newly risen shall be "taken up in the clouds to meet Christ;"[14] whence some commentators infer that the judgment will be held in the air.

c) Immediately before the second coming of Christ, "the sign of the Son of man" will appear in the heavens.[15] What may this sign be? Some Fathers think it is the cross on which our Saviour died, others, that a miraculous cross will appear in the air. Neither interpretation is certain.

d) Finally our Lord Himself will "come in the clouds of heaven with much power and majesty."[16]

e) All men without exception, the just as well as the wicked, will appear before His judgment seat. Matth. XXV, 32: "All nations shall be gathered together before him, and he shall separate them one from another, as the shepherd separateth the sheep from the goats."[17] Rom. XIV, 10: "We shall all stand before the judgment seat of Christ."[18]

Baptized infants who have done neither good nor evil will also appear, not, however, to be judged, but to behold the glory of the Judge.[19] The unbaptized will probably appear in order to be convinced of the justice of God in denying them the beatific vision.[20]

As for the pure spirits, the angels and demons, though they are already judged, they will participate in the General Judgment to receive the accidental rewards which

14 On the Eschatology of St. Paul see C. Lattey, S.J., in his appendix to Thessalonians in the Westminster Version, pp. 17 sqq.

15 Matth. XXIV, 30: "Et tunc parebit signum Filii hominis in caelo."

16 Ibid.: "Videbunt Filium hominis venientem in nubibus caeli cum virtute multa et maiestate."

17 Matth. XXV, 32: "Et congregabuntur ante eum omnes gentes, et separabit eos ab invicem, sicut pastor segregat oves ab hoedis."

18 Rom. XIV, 10: "Omnes enim stabimus ante tribunal Christi."

19 Cfr. St. Thomas, Summa Theol., Supplement., qu. 89, art. 5, ad 3: ". . . non ut iudicentur, sed ut videant gloriam iudicis."

20 Suarez.

they have merited or the punishments they have incurred by unduly influencing the course of human events.[21]

f) The twelve Apostles will sit in judgment over the tribes of Israel.[22] It is probable that the Blessed Virgin Mary, the prophets of the Old Testament, John the Baptist, and other saints will also assist the Great Judge.[23]

g) The judgment itself will embrace all the works of man, good and evil, thoughts, words, and deeds.[24] This is necessary to manifest the mysterious dispensations of Providence and the justice and glory of the Universal Judge.[25] It is prudent to hold with St. Thomas [26] and the majority of Catholic theologians that the forgiven secret sins of the just will also be revealed on the Last Day, in order that the judgment may be made complete and the justice and mercy of God glorified.

h) With regard to the form of the Last Judgment observe that such expressions as the separation of the goats from the sheep, the just standing on the right and the wicked on the left hand of the Judge, etc.,[27] may be allegorical. Their object probably is to show that the conduct and deserts of every man will become clearly apparent to his own conscience and to the whole world. To interpret these texts literally would hardly do, for the reason that, as St. Thomas points out,[28] such a process carried out literally would require an incalculable length of

21 Cfr. 1 Cor. VI, 3; 2 Pet. II, 4; Jude 6. (St. Thomas, *Summa Theol., Supplement.,* qu. 89, art. 8).

22 Matth. XIX, 28: *". . . vos qui secuti estis me, in regeneratione quum sederit Filius hominis in sede maiestatis suae, sedebitis et vos super sedes duodecim, iudicantes duodecim tribus Israel."* Cfr. 1 Cor. VI, 2: *"An nescitis quoniam sancti de hoc mundo iudicabunt?"*

23 Cfr. St. Thomas, *Summa Theol., Supplement.,* qu. 99, art. 2.

24 Cfr. Matth. XII, 36; 1 Cor. IV, 5.

25 Cfr. Suarez, *De Myst. Vitae Christi,* disp. 53, sect. 1.

26 *Supplement.,* qu. 87, art. 2.

27 Cfr. Matth. XXV, 32 sqq.

28 *Supplement.,* qu. 88, art. 2: *"Inaestimabilis magnitudo temporis ad hoc exigeretur."*

time.   Most probably the whole procedure will be over in a few minutes.   By divine illumination every man will instantly comprehend the state of his own soul and that of his fellow-creatures.   " It is likely," says St. Basil, " that by an inexpressible power, every deed we have done will be made manifest to us in a single moment, as if it were engraved on a tablet." [29]   The words of the sentence, however, " Come ye blessed," etc., will in all probability be actually spoken by Christ.

[29] *In Ioa.,* I, 18.

SECTION 2

CHILIASM, OR MILLENARIANISM

1. CHILIASM IN ITS TWO FORMS.—There are two forms of Chiliasm or Millenarianism. The exaggerated form is heretical, while the more moderate is simply erroneous.

a) The heretical form of Chiliasm may be traced partly to the Jewish expectation of a temporal Messias [1] and partly to the apocryphal writings of the Old Testament, which abound in fables.[2] The Chiliasts of this school conceived the millennium as a period of unbridled sensual indulgence. Eusebius the church-historian says of Cerinthus, a Gnostic heretic who flourished towards the end of the first century: " He held that at some time in the future Christ would reign on earth; and as he was addicted to the pleasures of the flesh, he imagined that the reign of God would consist of such things." [3] This error was shared by the ancient Ebionites and Apollinarianists and, in a somewhat more respectable form, still persists among the Mormons and Irvingites.

b) Moderate Chiliasm had a number of adherents among Patristic writers, notably Papias, Justin Martyr, Irenaeus, Tertullian, Nepos, Commodian, Victorinus of Pettau, and Lactantius. Its favorite text was Apoc.

---

1 Cfr. Is. IX, 6; LXVI, 18; Joel III, 17; Matth. XX, 20 sq.; Acts I, 6.   2 Cfr. Funk, *Patres Apostolici,* II, 276 sqq.   3 *Hist. Eccles.,* III, 28: " *Haec*

XX, 1 sqq.   Papias believed that the Resurrection of the flesh would be followed by a glorious reign of Christ, in which the Saints would enjoy a superabundance of earthly pleasures for a thousand years. These pleasures, however, were to be spiritual, or at least morally licit. In developing this idea its champions parted ways. Some expected the millennium between the General Judgment and the Resurrection of the dead, while others believed it would occur after the General Resurrection, immediately before the assumption of the just into Heaven. A third, still more moderate group of Millenarianists, which is not yet extinct, contents itself with asserting that an era of universal peace and tranquillity will precede the second coming of Christ, to be suddenly interrupted by the great apostasy and the forerunners of Anti-Christ.[4]

2. REFUTATION OF CHILIASM.—Chiliasm in both its forms is untenable.

a) Heretical Chiliasm stands condemned in the light of the moral law, which excludes intemperance and unchastity from the kingdom of Heaven.[5]   It is blasphemous and an insult to God to assert that Christ, who is all-holy, will found an earthly paradise for libertines. No wonder even those Fathers and ecclesiastical writers who entertained Chiliastic ideas vigorously condemned

fuit illius opinio, regnum Christi terrenum futurum. Et quarum rerum cupiditate ipse flagrabat, utpote voluptatibus corporis obnoxius carnique addictus, in eis regnum Dei situm fore somniavit."

4 On the modified Millenarianism of Chabauty (Avenir de l'Eglise

Catholique selon le Plan Divin, 1890) and Rohling (Erklärung der Apokalypse, 1895; Die Zukunft der Menschheit als Gattung, 1907) see Scheeben-Atzberger, Dogmatik, Vol. IV, 3, p. 908.

5 Cfr. Matth. XXII, 30; Rom. XIV, 17; 1 Cor. XV, 50 et passim

this grossly sensual species of Millenarianism as heretical.

b) It is not so easy to refute the more moderate form of Chiliasm, for it seems to have a basis in Sacred Scripture and primitive Tradition. The New Testament as well as the early creeds speak of the Resurrection of the flesh, the Last Judgment, and the end of the world in terms which make it apparent that these three events are to follow one another in close succession,[6] leaving no time for a millennium.

a) The favorite passage of the Chiliasts is in the Apocalypse and reads as follows: "And I beheld an angel coming down from heaven, holding in his hand the key of the bottomless pit, and a great chain. And he seized the dragon, the ancient serpent, who is the devil and Satan, and bound him for a thousand years. . . . They [i. e. the just] came to life again, and reigned with Christ for a thousand years. The rest of the dead came not to life until the thousand years were accomplished. This is the first resurrection. . . . And when the thousand years are accomplished, Satan shall be loosed from his prison, and he shall come forth to lead astray the nations which are in the four corners of the earth . . ."[7]

---

6 Cfr. John VI, 39; John XII, 48; Matth. XXIV, 14 sqq.; I Thess. IV, 15 sq.

7 Apoc. XX, 1 sqq.: "*Et vidi angelum descendentem de caelo, habentem clavem abyssi, et catenam magnam in manu sua. Et apprehendit draconem, serpentem antiquum, qui est diabolus, et satanas, et ligavit eum per annos mille* (χίλια ἔτη) *. . . Et vixerunt* [*iustorum animae*] *et regnaverunt cum Christo mille annis* (χίλια ἔτη). *Ceteri mortuorum non vixerunt, donec consummentur mille anni* (τὰ χίλια ἔτη): *haec est resurrectio prima. . . . Et quum consummati fuerint mille anni, solvetur satanas de carcere suo, et exibit, et seducet gentes, quae sunt super quattuor angulos terrae.*"

This is undeniably one of the most difficult and obscure passages found in Sacred Scripture, and no one has yet succeeded in explaining it satisfactorily. But it proves nothing in favor of Millenarianism, which has no claim to our assent unless it can show that its tenets do not conflict with the general teaching of the Bible. Among the more probable interpretations of the Johannine text suggested by Catholic writers we may mention that of St. Augustine, which was adopted by Pope St. Gregory the Great. These two Fathers think that the imprisonment of Satan refers to the first coming of our Lord, and his temporary loosing to His second coming (*parousia*) at the time of Antichrist. Christ's millennial reign with His saints on earth (the "first resurrection") signifies the kingdom of Heaven, where the Blessed reign under the headship of our Lord before the "second resurrection" (*i. e.* the Resurrection of the flesh). Similarly, the term "first death" is applied to the separation of the body from the soul, whereas "second death" refers to eternal damnation. If this theory is correct, the number one thousand is not to be taken literally, but simply indicates an indefinite period of considerable length.

β) Despite appearances to the contrary, Chiliasm has no foundation in Tradition. Among its early advocates Lactantius, Nepos, Commodian, and Victorinus may, in the light of the *Decretum Gelasianum,* be set aside as worthless witnesses.[8] The same could be said of Sulpicius Severus if he were to be reckoned among the Chiliasts, which is, however, extremely doubtful, as his extant writings contain no trace of this error. Of the remaining writers who are quoted in favor of Chiliasm we

8 The *Decretum de recipiendis et non recipiendis libris* is a series of papal decrees said to have been issued by St. Gelasius I at a Roman synod about A. D. 494. Cfr. Bardenhewer-Shahan, *Patrology,* p. 620; Mansi, *Collect. Concil.,* VIII, 151, 170.

may disregard Papias because he was uncritical,[9] and Tertullian because he was a heretic when he embraced Millenarianism.[10] St. Justin Martyr [11] and St. Irenaeus,[12] the only two remaining witnesses who are absolutely trustworthy, did not inculcate Chiliasm as an article of faith, but merely proposed it as a personal opinion. Whether St. Melito, Bishop of Sardes, harbored Millenarian notions, is uncertain.[13] St. Hippolytus, who is numbered among the Chiliasts by Bonwetsch,[14] has not written a single line, in the works that have come down to us, which must necessarily be interpreted in a Chiliastic sense.[15] Bonwetsch himself [16] is constrained to admit that Hippolytus discarded some of the eschatological notions held by Irenaeus and Tertullian.

Among the opponents of Chiliasm were Clemens Alexandrinus, Origen, and Dionysius, Bishop of Alexandria, whom Eusebius honored with the title of Great and St. Athanasius called a Doctor of the Catholic Church.[17]

READINGS : — J. B. Paganini, *Das Ende der Welt oder die Wiederkunft unseres Herrn*, 2nd ed., Ratisbon 1882.— J. Bautz, *Weltgericht und Weltende*, Mayence 1886.— J. Sigmund, *Das Ende der Zeiten mit einem Nachblick in die Ewigkeit, oder das Weltgericht mit seinen Ursachen, Vorzeichen und Folgen*, Salzburg 1892.— J. A. McHugh in the *Catholic Encyclopedia*, Vol. VIII, pp. 552 sq.— J. Tixeront, *History of Dogmas*, 3 Vols., St. Louis 1910-1916, see Index *s. v.* "Judgment."— St. Thomas, *S. Theol., Supplem.*, qu. 49-91.

9 Cfr. Eusebius, *Hist. Eccles.*, III, 39, 11.
10 Cfr. Tertullian, *Adv. Marcion.*, III, 24.
11 *Dial. c. Tryph.*, c. 80 sq.
12 *Adv. Haer.*, V, 32 sqq.
13 Cfr. Bardenhewer, *Geschichte der altkirchlichen Literatur*, Vol. I, p. 551, Freiburg 1902.
14 *Hippol. Opera*, pp. 243 sq., Leipsic 1897.

15 Cfr. Atzberger, *Geschichte der christlichen Eschatologie innerhalb der vornizänischen Zeit*, pp. 278 sqq., Freiburg 1896.
16 *Studien zu den Kommentaren Hippolyts*, p. 50, Leipsic 1897.
17 Eusebius, *Hist. Eccles.*, VI, 35; VII, *praef.*; St. Athanasius, *Ep. de Sent. Dion.*, c. 6. Cfr. Bardenhewer-Shahan, *Patrology*, p. 154.

On Chiliasm see H. Corrodi, *Kritische Geschichte des Chilias-mus*, 1794.— H. Klee, *De Chiliasmo Primorum Saeculorum*, May-ence 1825.— Wagner, *Der Chiliasmus in den ersten Jahrhunderten*, 1849.— J. N. Schneider, *Die chiliastische Doktrin und ihr Ver-hältnis zur christlichen Glaubenslehre* (pro-Chiliastic), Schaff-hausen 1859.— J. P. Kirsch, art. "Millennium," in Vol. X of the *Catholic Encyclopedia*, pp. 307-310.— Chiapelli, *Le Idee Millenarie dei Cristiani*, Naples 1888.— L. Guy, *Le Millénarisme dans ses Ori-gines et son Développement*, Paris 1904.— Franzelin, *De Scriptura et Traditione*, P. II, thes. 16, Rome 1896.— H. Kihn, *Patrologie*, Vol. I, pp. 120 sqq., Paderborn 1904.— J. Tixeront, *History of Dogmas*, Vol. I, St. Louis 1910 (see Index *s. v.* "Millenarian-ism").

ACKNOWLEDGMENT

The Editor begs leave to express his gratitude for valuable assistance rendered in the preparation of this series, to the Rt. Rev. Abbot Charles Mohr, O.S.B., D.D., of St. Leo, Fla.; the V. Rev. Bernard J. Otting, S.J., President of St. Louis University; the Rev. James A. Kleist, S.J., of Campion College, Prairie du Chien, Wis., and the Rev. A. J. Wolfgarten, D.D., Ph.D., of the Ca-thedral College, Chicago, Ill.

INDEX

A

"Abraham's bosom," 26.
Acts of the Martyrs, 27.
Adam, 6, 11, 12.
Aërius, 77.
Agility as an endowment of the glorified body, 146 sq.
Albigenses, 78, 122.
Alexander VII, 90.
Ambrose, St., 10, 58, 86, 130.
Amor beatificus, 31.
Angels, 36, 92, 93, 99, 151, 152, 157.
Anselm, St., 119.
Antichrist, 109 sqq., 156, 158.
Apocalypse, 8 sq., 33, 47, 66, 73, 133, 155 sq., 157.
Apocatastasis, 67 sqq., 122 sq.
Apostasy, The great, 109 sq.
Apostles, 153.
Apostles' Creed, 39, 92, 122.
Appollinarianists, 155.
Armenian heretics, 131.
Athanasian Creed, 65, 122, 132.
Athanasius, St., 159.
Athenagoras, 130.
Augustine, St., 5 sq., 8, 10, 12, 14, 20 sq., 33, 40, 42, 58, 65, 68, 71, 81, 86, sq., 97, 102, 105, 136, 142, 158.
Aureolæ, 43.

B

Baptism, 94 sq.
Barnabas, Epistle of, 151.
Basil, St., 58, 81, 154.
Beatitude, 29 sqq., 52.
Bellarmine, Card., 36, 88, 96, 100.
Benedict XII, 23, 24, 32, 39.
Bessarion, Card., 85.

Body, Nature of the risen, 138 sqq.; Identity of, 140 sqq.; Four transcendent qualities of, 144 sqq.
Boëthius, 29.
Bonaventure, St., 15, 84.
Bonwetsch, 159.
" Book of Judgment," 18 sq.
Braun, Charles (S.J.), 118.
Brightness as a quality of the glorified body, 145 sq.
Burying the dead, 96.

C

Calvin, 19, 78, 82.
Catharinus, Ambrose, 56.
Cerinthus, 155.
Chiliasm, 19, 22, 149, 151, 155 sqq.
Chrysostom, St., 19, 25, 48, 49, 51, 54, 68, 95, 112.
Clement of Alexandria, St., 87, 88, 130, 159.
Clement of Rome, St., 131, 134.
Commodian, 155, 158.
Communion of Saints, 36, 92 sqq.
Compenetrabilitas, 148.
Conflagration, The universal, 117 sqq.
Constantinople, Council of (543), 65; (553), 65, 122 sq.
Consummation of the world, 1, 2.
Cosmas Indicopleustes, 50.
Cremation, 96.
Cyprian, St., 14, 26, 69.
Cyril of Jerusalem, St., 97, 131.

D

Dante, 49, 74.

161

Deo gratias!